THE RHETORIC
OF ANTINUCLEAR
FICTION

THE RHETORIC OF ANTINUCLEAR FICTION

Persuasive Strategies in Novels and Films

Patrick Mannix

Lewisburg
Bucknell University Press
London and Toronto: Associated University Presses

Associated University Presses
440 Forsgate Drive
Cranbury, NJ 08512

Associated University Presses
25 Sicilian Avenue
London WC1A 2QH, England

Associated University Presses
P.O. Box 39, Clarkson Pstl. Stn.
Mississauga, Ontario,
L5J 3X9 Canada

The paper used in this publication meets the requirements of the American National Standard for Permanence of Paper for Printed Library Materials Z39.48-1984.

Library of Congress Cataloging-in-Publication Data

Mannix, Patrick, 1952–
    The rhetoric of antinuclear fiction : persuasive strategies in
novels and films / Patrick Mannix.
        p.   cm.
    Based on the author's thesis (Ohio State University).
    Includes bibliographical references (p.   ) and index.
    ISBN 0-8387-5218-7 (alk. paper)
    1. American fiction—20th century—History and criticism.
2. Nuclear warfare and literature—United States.   3. Antinuclear
movement—United States.   4. Antinuclear movement in literature.
5. Nuclear warfare in motion pictures.   6. Peace movements—United
States.   7. Peace movements in literature.   8. Persuasion (Rhetoric)
I. Title.
PS374.N82M36   1992
813'.5409358—dc20   91-55466
                                                                        CIP

PRINTED IN THE UNITED STATES OF AMERICA

To my parents
with love and gratitude

Contents

Preface

Whatever else it has done for or to human history, the twentieth century has increased dramatically the pace at which inevitable change overtakes us. With dizzying speed, yesterday's enemy becomes today's ally, and today's certainties turn into tomorrow's imponderables.

When I first began to study the fiction of nuclear war in 1984, the Cold War seemed a reliable, if depressing, constant. Both of the major powers were increasing their nuclear arsenals in Western Europe; Leonid Brezhnev was ruling the Soviet Union with a resolute devotion to the past; and Ronald Reagan was touting the benefits of an elaborate missile defense system to stave off the depraved intentions of "the Evil Empire." By 1990, as I was revising this manuscript for publication, relations between the two countries had improved so much that many people rather indelicately wondered out loud to me whether such a work still had any relevance.

While admitting to the possibility of some bias, I have always dismissed such speculation. For one thing, whatever the state of the nuclear threat at the moment, it has held the human race hostage for almost half a century. And the fiction that is at issue in this work needs no greater claim on our attention than its attempt to deal with that threat. A sudden outbreak of international amicability may make a study of antinuclear fiction seem a bit less urgent, but it doesn't make such a study any less important.

Moreover, we may question just how defunct the nuclear threat really is. *Glasnost* notwithstanding, none of the nuclear powers has made a move to begin reducing their arsenals. In 1985, William M. Arkin and Richard W. Fieldhouse in *Nuclear Battlefields* estimated that the various nuclear powers had fifty to sixty thousand nuclear warheads deployed around the world.[1] About the same number are in place as I write this preface in the early part of 1991.

At the same time, recent events have reminded us how easily the same international volatility that brought the world to the brink of peace in the first place can just as easily send it spinning

9

off toward chaos. The very instability in the Soviet system that produced *glasnost* has led to a dangerous power struggle in the Soviet Union. We cannot be sure what forces will ultimately prevail in this struggle, but we can be sure that they will end up controlling a good portion of the world's nuclear arsenal.

We have even been given some reason to wonder just how thorough changes in the Soviet outlook have been. Some of those in the West who hailed Mikhail Gorbachev as a liberal reformer found themselves looking on with concern as he attempted to assume virtually dictatorial powers during 1990. And the decisiveness with which Soviet troops moved to suppress independence movements in the Baltic states in 1991 looked to many like Cold War business as usual.

Even if we do stand on the brink of a new era of peace and cooperation between the Soviet Union and the rest of the world, however, enough other dangers exist to make us uneasy about the still extant nuclear arsenal. The Chinese, for example, control about three hundred warheads, more than enough to throw a fatal spark into the nuclear powder keg.[2] And who can feel confident that the architects of the Tiananmann Square massacre would not use such firepower as some last desperate resort if they began to feel that history was slipping through their fingers?

As far as the West is concerned, the perceived evaporation of the danger of World War III threatens to revive the concept of nuclear intimidation as a viable method of dealing with international problems. As the Persian Gulf crisis of 1990–1991 came to a boil, many Americans publicly wondered why the United States didn't meet Saddam Hussein's aggression against Kuwait with a nuclear attack rather than with a massive deployment of conventional forces. The fact that such an issue would be raised at all suggests a dangerous slippage in the horror of nuclear use that had developed through the forty-five years of the Cold War.

Finally the possibility that some sort of nuclear threat could arise in the third world cannot be dismissed. In the Middle East, Israel is widely believed to have nuclear weapons while various Arab nations—most notably Iraq—have attempted to develop a nuclear capacity. Given this trend, the future of that very troubled area could well hold a small-scale, but still potentially disastrous, reproduction of the Soviet-American arms race.

I don't wish to discount entirely the hopes that recent events have spawned, but I do wish to suggest that our celebration of the end of the nuclear era is premature. So, too, is any tendency to conclude that antinuclear fiction has had its final say. The nuclear dilemma will take many twists and turns before it is done with us, and antinuclear fiction will continue to remind us of the danger we face. Indeed, to the extent that new hopes have lulled us into complacency about nuclear weapons, antinuclear fiction may assume an even greater role in the effort to end the nuclear threat.

Such an end will come only as more of us finally appreciate—emotionally as well as intellectually—the level of jeopardy that nuclear weapons continue to represent for us. I would be pleased if, in a small way, this book—by examining efforts to make that jeopardy emotionally palpable—can contribute to such an appreciation. Whether that hope is reasonable or not, I am confident that the works I examine here have added to the public's appreciation of the nuclear threat, and that these and other works employing the same or similar rhetorical strategies will continue to do so.

I would like to take this opportunity to acknowledge the help and support various people have offered during my work on this project. First, I thank Professors Edward P. J. Corbett and Christian Zacher of Ohio State University for their advice as I was writing the dissertation on which the present work is based and for their encouragement about the prospects of turning that dissertation into a book. I also thank Professor Leonard A. Podis of Oberlin College for advising me on some later revisions. A very special thanks goes to Vincent Casaregola, Jeanne Colleran, and Charles Zarobila for listening to me, encouraging me, and generally helping to sustain my spirit throughout the project. Finally, and most importantly, I thank my family for their boundless love and support.

This work grew out of a dissertation, *Available Means: Manifestations of Aristotle's Three Modes of Appeal in Anti-Nuclear Fiction*, ©1987 by Patrick James Mannix.

THE RHETORIC
OF ANTINUCLEAR
FICTION

1
Rhetoric and Fiction

An entire generation has been born and has grown to maturity since the development of the atomic bomb. We who are members of that generation have lived our entire lives in a world weighted with the trappings of the nuclear age. During the 1950s, my brother and sister scrambled under their school desks for "duck and cover" air-raid drills and wore dog tags so their charred bodies could be identified if the "unthinkable" occurred. By the time I entered school, these particular signs of the times had disappeared, but my classmates and I daily marched to recess beneath the yellow and black fallout shelter signs next to the doors of the school. I also remember flipping through Civil Defense pamphlets that told, in simple prose illustrated with stick-figure drawings, how to avoid death or serious injury from nuclear war even if you happened to be caught in open country by the attack. All the while, news reports kept reminding us of the reasons for the drills and the pamphlets and all the rest by recording each technological advance that made the world an increasingly dangerous place to be: the hydrogen bomb in the early 1950s, the intercontinental ballistic missile in the early 1960s, the neutron bomb and the cruise missile in the 1970s, and the specter of "Star Wars" in the 1980s.

With each of these advances we were treated—or subjected—to a new round of the ongoing debate between those who opposed the further development of nuclear weapons and those who saw in that development the only hope for peace and freedom in the world. As much as the bomb itself, that debate became a significant part of the environment in which we matured. Even the least politically astute of us were aware of its concerns playing at the edges of our consciousness. Its terminology seeped into our everyday conversation: we began to speak of a difficult situation's having fallout instead of consequences; when we desired the ultimate defeat of an opponent—whether on the playing field or in the board room—we might urge our associates to "nuke 'em";

in our fascination with the bikini bathing suit, we unconsciously memorialized one of the first atomic test sites.

Given the degree to which concern about nuclear weapons has permeated our consciousness, we should not be surprised to realize that American popular culture for the past forty years exhibits a recurring fascination with the possibility of nuclear war. The bomb has played a starring role in a dizzying variety of novels, films, plays, and television programs. To be sure, many of these works have used nuclear destruction merely as a plot device—as the ultimate danger that James Bond must thwart or the cataclysm that has produced the chaos through which Mad Max glumly stalks. To the extent that this is true, popular culture has helped to trivialize the problem of nuclear weapons, much as it has frequently trivialized the horrors of the Third Reich by dredging up the reliable Nazi villain to add menace to some standard melodrama.

But just as popular culture has at times set out to explore the true horrors of Nazi Germany, it has also recurrently turned its attention to purposeful attacks on the dangers of nuclear weapons. Indeed, I have found over one hundred works—an average of more than two per year of the nuclear age—that attack nuclear weapons to some significant extent. Many of these works have long since faded into obscurity. Titles like *The Hearth, Millennium, Five,* and *Level 7* are now known only to a handful of devotees of science fiction or apocalyptic literature. Other works, however— *On the Beach, Dr. Strangelove, The Day After*—remain in our collective consciousness and probably will do so for some time to come.

Yet little has been done to examine how such works go about their task or to establish the relationship between the ongoing nuclear debate in society and fictional attempts to sway that debate. To my knowledge no full-length treatment of the persuasive strategies of antinuclear fiction has ever been made. This book is an attempt to provide such a treatment.

It is not, however, a chronological history of antinuclear fiction, either in novels or in films. Nor is it intended to be what most theorists would think of as an ideological analysis of the subject. Rather, it is an attempt to describe the range of more or less conscious strategies employed by the creators of various works of fiction designed to arouse public antipathy for the development and deployment of nuclear weapons.

The general organizing principle I use in the study as a whole relies on a classification of persuasive—or rhetorical—appeals into basically three types: the ethical, the rational, and the emotional.

The concept of the three persuasive appeals is as old as Aristotle's *Rhetoric* and as contemporary as the most recent college composition textbook. It is based on the idea that any communicative act necessarily involves three main components: the communicator, the material he communicates, and the audience to whom he is communicating. Conveniently, each of the three major modes of rhetorical appeal concerns itself with one of these components. The ethical appeal is the confidence that the character of the communicator inspires. The rational, of course, is the substance of the case the communicator makes. The emotional centers on the reactions of the audience and aims at bending those reactions to the cause at hand.

One need not delve deeply into rhetorical theory, however, to appreciate the concept of the three modes of persuasive appeal. Our everyday lives constantly provide examples of all three. The advertising industry has long seen the value of the ethical appeal by paying celebrities to serve as spokespeople for products. They know that when Robert Young advises the jittery residents of television land to drink a certain brand of decaffeinated coffee, his very presence will suggest the caring concern of the father who knew best and the medical expertise of Dr. Marcus Welby. Many in the audience will be disposed to trust his opinion simply because of these implied character traits.

A similar dynamic applies, of course, when the source quoted is more authoritative. If we are told that three out of four doctors recommend a certain pain reliever, we tend to believe in the worth of the product because we assume doctors know a good pain reliever when they see one. When President Kennedy suggested that it was possible to fly a man to the moon, he succeeded in marshaling the resources of the nation behind the project because the American taxpayers concluded that, as president, he was privy to classified data that proved the project feasible. During the congressional investigation of the Iran-Contra Affair in the spring of 1987, Fawn Hall stated that she helped Oliver North shred sensitive documents because she respected him and knew he must have a good reason for his actions.

And there is the rub, for Ms. Hall's allegiance to the charismatic Colonel North exemplifies a major pitfall of the ethical appeal: those who blindly follow a strong leader may end up in some kind of trouble. Aristotle himself pointed out that the ethical appeal depends on the audience's perception of the sterling character of the speaker, not necessarily on the validity of that perception. People can be deluded into trusting someone who is actually working purely in his own self-interest or a well-earned respect for someone may generate such loyalty that people will follow him uncritically even when he is wrong. History provides no end of examples of either dynamic.

Of course, as far as the communicator is concerned, the vulnerability of the audience to a strong ethical appeal is no problem. If his listeners are inclined to follow him blindly, so much the better. But some members of the audience, perhaps remembering past abuses of the ethical appeal, may be reluctant to follow the charismatic leader uncritically. Frequently and unfairly called cynics, they may insist on scrutinizing the substance of the communicator's case. They demand that the evidence be laid out for them so that they can make their own informed choice about whether the proposed course of action is indeed the best. They demand a rational appeal.

Actually, very few people will do something simply because someone tells them to. Life is not really a game of "Simon Says" nor are people actually lemmings ready to rush to their own destruction on command. Presumably even those who are too lazy or uninformed to examine the facts of a case do demand at least the implicit assurance that the person whose advice or orders they are following arrived at *his* conclusions through some rational process. And usually people will demand at least a *pro forma* argument from even the wisest and most trusted leader.

Therefore, anyone who really wants to persuade an audience will necessarily have to pay some attention to the message he offers—will have to give some nod to the rational appeal. For all their reliance on slogans, sound bites, and sixty second commercials, politicians do ultimately feel some pressure to talk about the issues. A whole genre of "Just the facts ma'am" commercials presents talking heads who extol the virtues of particular products without benefit of fancy imagery or dazzling editing. Even Robert Young must say *something* substantive about his coffee.

But, like the ethical appeal, the rational appeal has potential drawbacks. One is quite simply that the rational appeal is difficult. Although most people like to think that they behave rationally and claim to respect a logical appeal, they are too often reluctant to expend the effort required to sift through arguments and issues when they are actually faced with a decision. We probably don't have to look much farther than the latest election to appreciate this point. Few of those in the 40 percent of the electorate who take the trouble to vote at all go through an entire ballot confident that they know enough about each candidate and issue to make a completely rational choice.

A more central problem of the rational appeal, however, is the fact that, by its very nature, it is aimed at the head and not at the heart. While this quality may increase the chances that truth will out, it does not necessarily indicate that the audience will respond to that truth. In other words, we may assent to the value of a proposed course of action, but if acting on that assent would require us to change some cherished aspect of our lives, we may decline to follow the path that logic urges. This point is familiar to anyone who has ever attempted to break a bad habit. A smoker, for example, can admit the validity of all the objective evidence that he is ruining his health, but that assent does not necessarily make him stop smoking. He may need a more potent motivator, and that might be provided by an emotional appeal.

Again, we need not look far to see how much power—for better or worse—our emotions exercise over our actions. The Japanese attack on Pearl Harbor in 1941 helped spark an anger and a patriotism in the American public that carried them through four years of extreme sacrifice to defeat the Axis powers during World War II. When news programs began televising images of the starving in Ethiopia during the 1980s, people were so moved to pity that contributions to organizations working to counteract the famine in that country increased dramatically. The stock market crash of October 1987 has been attributed, at least in part, to unreasoning panic. Fear of AIDS has contributed to a resurgence of fidelity in sexual relationships but at the same time has promoted often brutally hostile acts against people who have the disease—or who are suspected of having it. I could, of course, add endlessly to this list. We are all familiar with how our emotions can significantly affect our actions—sometimes in collaboration with rational judgment, sometimes in active opposition to that judgment.

Indeed, it sometimes seems that people are more likely to be driven by emotion than by reason. Certainly the widespread use of emotional appeals in persuasive efforts suggests that those who are charged with influencing public opinion—advertising executives, media consultants, and so on—pay special attention to the power of the emotions. The average car commercial, for example, doesn't simply offer a means of transportation—often enough it doesn't really talk about transportation at all. Instead, it attempts to seduce the potential buyer with talk of "power," "performance," and "sleek lines." For good measure the ad frequently throws in an enticing woman to cast yearning glances toward the viewer's surrogate as he slides behind the wheel, or—in a nod to feminism—allows the woman the assertiveness to slip behind the wheel herself and peel away from her hapless and hopelessly outclassed male admirer. The fantasy plays to the emotions—to that part of us that wants to be sexier and more powerful than we actually perceive ourselves to be. In doing so, the ad may succeed in overriding our reason, which might tell us that a station wagon might be a more prudent choice for our family.

We are constantly subjected to this dynamic. We have a primal urge to protect our loved ones, so a burglar alarm company treats us to the sight of a brutal man breaking into a house where a woman and some children cower in terror. We have a natural desire to feel secure in the present and to have hope for the future, so the political party in power tells us that "America is standing tall," and that "It's morning in America." We have an almost instinctive compassion for the suffering of our fellow man, and the other party tells us that an unfeeling government has abandoned the poor and the homeless. For good and for ill, fairly and unfairly, those who would move us to action—or lull us into inaction—fall back on the emotional appeal.

I don't wish to leave the impression, however, that these appeals necessarily work in opposition to—or even in isolation from—one another. All three appeals can be used to support each other in a single persuasive effort. In fact, it is probably impossible to perform a persuasive act without employing all three types of appeal, explicitly or implicitly, consciously or unconsciously. A person will necessarily project a certain character when he speaks or writes, and his audience will inevitably adopt some attitude toward him and his message on the basis of that projection. And even if the speaker or writer is determined to use logic to convince his audience, his logical argument will probably move the listeners' emotions if it is to be at all effective.

Of course, many theorists might raise questions about the validity of studying the rhetorical strategies of antinuclear fiction, denying that artistic endeavors in general *can* affect political or social attitudes. At the very least they might insist that such effects ought not to be of concern to those who study art. Clearly the fact that literature and rhetoric have long been studied separately in universities, frequently in different departments, seems to reflect a widely held belief that the methods of persuasion have little bearing on the study of fiction.

When critics *have* applied rhetoric to literary works, they have generally done so more to explain how artistic effects are achieved than to examine how the work succeeds as a persuasive medium. For example, rhetoric has frequently provided the tools for examinations of style in literary works. On occasion, principles of argumentation have been cited to demonstrate how a work has been structured. Only rarely have critics examined literature as rhetoric: Edward P. J. Corbett's explication of "A Modest Proposal," and Sheldon Sacks's *Fiction and the Shape of Belief* being two notable examples. Generally academic criticism has traditionally preserved a more or less strict separation between rhetoric and literature.

But the concept that literature can have a significant rhetorical function once had an honored place in the critical tradition. In an essay entitled "Poetry as Instrument," in fact, O. G. Brockett states that until about 1800, the dominant view of literature was that its mission was to teach pleasurably.[1] This is to say that for upwards of two thousand years in Western society, literature was seen, at least in part, as a specialized rhetorical instrument. This concept received its most unequivocal early form in the *Ars Poetica* of Horace who counseled, "Poets wish either to profit or delight, or to combine enjoyment and usefulness when they write. . . . He who combines teaching with enjoyment carries the day by at the same time delighting and admonishing the reader."[2]

The view that literature had a legitimate persuasive function became the cornerstone of the first great critical work in the English language, Sir Philip Sidney's "Defense of Poesy." Written in the late sixteenth century, the treatise is an attempt to defend the art of literature from charges of frivolity and immorality. To uphold the value of poetry, Sidney falls back on Horace's dictum. He defines poetry as "an art of imitation, for so Aristotle termeth it in the word *mimesis*, that is to say a representing, counterfeiting, or figuring forth—to speak metaphorically, a speaking picture, with this end, to teach and delight."[3] Whatever the immediate end of poetry may be, he adds, "The final end is to lead and draw us to as high a perfection as our degenerate souls, made worse by their clay lodgings, can be capable of."[4]

For nearly two centuries after Sidney, English critics continued to maintain the importance of the persuasive function of literature. It was only in the late eighteenth and early nineteenth centuries that the Horatian formula was largely supplanted by what M. H. Abrams calls the "expressive" view of literature. In *The Mirror and the Lamp* he describes the general qualities of the

critical theories of Wordsworth, Coleridge, Shelley, and other
romantic writers: "The paramount cause of poetry is not, as in
Aristotle, a formal cause, . . . nor, as in neo-classical criticism, a
final cause, the effect intended upon the audience; but instead an
efficient cause—the impulse within the poet of feelings and de-
sires seeking expression, or the compulsion of the 'creative' imagination which, like God the creator, has its internal source of
motion."[5]

Naturally, such an approach to literature necessarily deem-
phasizes any rhetorical function of literature. From the point of
view of the romantic author or critic, a literary work is valuable
because it reveals the soul of its creator, and the function of
criticism is to help illuminate that revelation. Still, even romantics
recognized that the self-expression of the author might have some
useful effect on the reader. Wordsworth, himself, explicitly addresses this point:

> For our continued influxes of feelings are modified and directed by
> our thoughts . . . so, by the repetition and continuance of this act, our
> feelings will be connected with important subjects, till at length . . .
> such habits of mind will be produced, that, by obeying blindly and
> mechanically the impulses of those habits, we shall describe objects,
> and utter sentiments, of such a nature . . . that the understanding of
> the Reader must necessarily be in some degree enlightened, and his
> affections strengthened and purified.[6]

Much of the same attitude seems to form the foundation of
Shelley's statement, "Poets are the unacknowledged legislators of
the world."[7] Nevertheless, the romantic movement signaled a
crucial shift away from the traditional rhetorical view of literature.

Subsequent developments in literature and literary theory wid-
ened the rift between fiction and rhetoric. The aesthetic movement of the late nineteenth century declared independence from
rhetorical demands by proclaiming that art existed for art's sake
alone, rather than for the moral improvement of individuals or
societies. This theory gave impetus during the first half of the
twentieth century to various formalist orientations toward literature, most notably the New Criticism, which held sway over an
entire generation of English teachers.

The New Critics insisted that the whole of a work's meaning—
the whole of its importance and value—could be found in the text
itself. So complete was their faith in the absolute integrity of the
text that they explicitly excluded the intention of the author and

the effect on the audience from the realm of the critic's concern. In fact, in *The Verbal Icon* William K. Wimsatt and Monroe C. Beardsley coined the terms "Intentional Fallacy" and "Affective Fallacy" to condemn such concerns.

Such a view necessarily ignores—at least on the theoretical level—a consideration of the work as an attempt to communicate a specific message from the author to the reader. In practice, however, considerations about what an individual work might be "saying" were somewhat difficult to ignore absolutely, even for a New Critic. James L. Kinneavy, who himself adopts a formalist view of literature in *A Theory of Discourse,* admits as much: "It is, of course, undeniably true that literature does communicate meaning. This is necessarily so because literature uses words as its artistic material, just as painting uses color and lines, and words refer to reality, they have meaning. Further, many of these meanings are usually marshalled by a unified ordering into what is normally called 'theme.' "[8]

This inability of New Criticism to banish theme from literature leaves open the possibility of examining fiction from a specifically rhetorical standpoint. If someone makes a statement, the person who reads it will either affirm or deny it. If the reader affirms the statement, the author has succeeded rhetorically. The most a New Critic could do would be to say that the work has ceased to function as literature when such a rhetorical act is occurring. But such a distinction would be academic. Since the New Critic maintains that a work is complete in itself and unchanging, it would still be a work of literature even if it were being used rhetorically. A wrench is still a wrench even if someone uses it to hammer nails.

Post-New Critical movements posed even greater obstacles to the champion of rhetorical criticism by placing the meaning of a work outside the text or even by attacking accepted notions of the very possibility of conveying meaning through language. Structuralism, for example, parallels New Criticism by limiting its examination of literature to form, but it does so by seeking beyond the individual artifact to discover the deep formal structures of all works. It attempts to identify generic or archetypal blueprints to which all works—or least all works of a certain type—conform. As Raman Selden points out in *Contemporary Literary Theory.* "Not only the text but also the author is canceled as the structuralist places in brackets the actual work and the person who wrote it, in order to isolate the true object of enquiry—the system."[9] Clearly such an approach gives little support to the rhetorical critic for whom the capacity of an individual utterance to convey an author's intention effectively to an actual audience is paramount.

While various reader-oriented critical schools reintroduce into literary theory the rhetorically vital component of audience response, they also tend to strike at the heart of a rhetorical approach by maintaining that the meaning of a work is found, not in the author's intention but in the reader's (or the reading community's) act of interpretation. Stanley Fish makes this point in *Is There a Text in This Class?* "Whereas I had once agreed with my predecessors on the need to control interpretation lest it overwhelm and obscure texts, facts, authors, and intentions, I now believe that interpretation is the source of texts, facts, authors, and intentions. Or to put it another way, the entities that were once seen as competing for the right to constrain interpretation (text, reader, author) are now all seen to be the *products* of interpretation."[10] Clearly, this insistence that the meaning of a work is not primarily the product of the author's attempt to communicate with the reader through the text but rather the result of the reading community's acts of interpretation of the text seems to undercut the concept that fiction can perform as rhetoric.

On an even more extreme level, deconstructionists take a theoretical axe to the very foundations of rhetorical views of fiction by attacking not olny the ability of the text to make stable referential statements about anything but also the concept that there is any stable meaning to refer to. Denying the existence of any essential truth that stands outside of language and provides its foundation, the deconstructionist asserts that all "truth" is simply the product of language itself. But the lack of any foundation makes language ultimately indeterminate and, therefore, unable to make stable referential statements about anything. Speaking of Anglo-American deconstruction, Terry Eagleton notes, "Literary criticism thus becomes an ironic, uneasy business, an unsettling venture into the inner void of the text which lays bare the illusoriness of meaning, the impossibility of truth and the deceitful guiles of all discourse."[11] Such a concept poses obvious difficulties for the rhetorical critic—not to mention the rhetorical writer.

Of course, we have neither the time nor the space here for anything like a thorough debate over the implications of the various critical theories I have alluded to. I would like to suggest, however, that many of the apparent difficulties that some critical theories of the past two hundred years pose to rhetorical criticism are the results of a kind of theoretical tunnel vision. Literary communication, like any other form of discourse, is a complex process that depends on cooperative interaction between the writer and the audience through the text. To the extent that any critical school tends to overemphasize the role of any one of these elements in its approach to the communicative act, it distorts our understanding of that act.

A. P. Foulkes, relying on semiotician Charles Morris's model of the communication process, makes this point in his book *Literature and Propaganda:*

> Schools of criticism, which in Morris's sense function as "descriptions of aspects of a complex process" claiming to be "rival accounts of the whole process", distort the model by introducing hierarchies of inter-pretant, the purpose of which is often to create rules regarding valida-tion procedures, admissibility of evidence and so on. Interestingly, twentieth-century criticism has moved steadily across the model . . . biographical emphasis was dislodged by various text-related methods such as New Criticism, while more recently these methods have been replaced by a criticism based on reader-response.[12]

Thus, expressive views of literature are problematical to the extent that they downgrade the importance of audience. Reader-based theories, on the other hand, are lacking in that they banish au-thorial intent from critical consideration. The failure of New Crit-icism is not its advocacy of textual analysis, but its insistence on excluding both author and audience from the critical mix.

Many structuralist and poststructuralist theories of language and literature raise thornier problems because their challenges to the kind of rhetorical analysis I deal with here ultimately rest on basic assumptions about the nature of humanity, the nature of human consciousness, and the nature of the world. Besides again being beyond the scope of this work, a debate on such issues would be ultimately pointless. We cannot demonstrate the exis-tence—or nonexistence—of stable, external, even metaphysical foundations of truth. We can neither "prove" nor "disprove" the existence of the human soul, of God, of preexistent ideas or of any of the other traditional foundations of such truths. These issues are, in the end, matters of belief.

It is probably evident that my own beliefs lead me toward what would be labeled a broadly humanist view of the world and of discourse. And the rhetorical approach I employ here reflects those assumptions. It seeks to preserve a sense of balance among various entities—author, audience, text, and the world—main-taining that it is in that balance that the true, living meaning of any utterance lies. Indeed, the three rhetorical appeals around which I structure this study correspond directly to the first three of these factors. And implicit in rhetoric's concern with effective persuasion and communication is its conviction that discourse significantly influences—and is influenced by—the world in which it is carried out. While any given rhetorical analysis may concentrate on one or another aspect of the process, it always, at least implicitly, sees that part in relation to the others.

Such an approach seems especially appropriate when we are faced with fiction that is itself explicitly rhetorical. For whatever critical theory says about the desirability—or possibility—of literature's having a persuasive intent, it is difficult to deny that in practice authors *have* consciously attempted to use it as a rhetorical tool. The Christian Bible, for example, contains a number of stories—the book of Job, the parables of Jesus, and so forth—that have a moral point. Aristophanes's plays are satires that attack the follies of mankind in order to shame people into changing their behavior. Medieval European theater consisted largely of religious plays that taught doctrine and morals to the illiterate masses. Many of Chaucer's tales were exempla designed to teach some moral lesson to his readers. Edmund Spenser designed his *Faerie Queene* as a courtesy book to teach the ways of the gentleman. Generations of schoolchildren were raised on John Bunyan's *Pilgrim's Progress*, a legendary allegory about man's search for salvation.

Even after the cutting edge of critical theory had begun to move away from the concept that literature had an instructive function, the practice of teaching through fiction remained strong. The most notable instance of this phenomenon in the United States may be Harriet Beecher Stowe's *Uncle Tom's Cabin*. The success of the novel in raising abolitionist sentiment in the North was so great that, upon meeting Stowe, Abraham Lincoln jokingly remarked that she was "the little woman who made this great war."[13] Without beginning to exhaust the field, we could add such names as James Russell Lowell, Edward Bellamy, Upton Sinclair, John Dos Passos, and John Steinbeck to the list of American writers who have urged some specific social or political action in their fiction. A random list of reform-minded English authors might include Samuel Butler, Charles Dickens, George Bernard Shaw, and George Orwell.

And if we look to contemporary popular literature, our impression of the survival of the instructive function of fiction grows even stronger. Any novel by James Michener or Arthur Hailey seems to exist as much to give information as to provide entertainment. Despite one old movie mogul's supposed comment that messages should be sent by Western Union rather than by 20th Century Fox or MGM, theatrical films—from *The Grapes of Wrath* to *The China Syndrome*—have recurrently attempted to make serious statements about contemporary social problems. Television, with its lineup of socially oriented films on subjects ranging from incest to international politics to euthanasia, might well change the title *Movie of the Week* to *Issue of the Week*.

The works I will examine in this book lie firmly within this tradition. Each has, as a major part of its purpose, at least an implicit intention to affect its audience's attitudes toward nuclear war. To be sure, some hold this purpose more centrally than others. The agendas of works like *Riddley Walker* and *Dr. Strangelove* are more complicated than those of *Level 7* or *The Day After*. Still, all can be profitably studied as attempts at persuasion.

What follows then is an overview of the dominant strategies of antinuclear fiction, focusing on the uses of the ethical, rational, and emotional appeals. To each I devote two chapters, the first of which analyzes how the appeal seems to work in fiction in general. While I have based these analyses primarily on personal experience and observation, I do not claim to be breaking any startling theoretical ground with them. Indeed, the points I make are so much based on common sense that I would be surprised if they had not been made in various places before. The only reason for their inclusion here is to smooth the present reader's path into the second chapter of each set which details the particular manifestations of the appeals in antinuclear fiction.

Following this survey of the workings of each mode of appeal in antinuclear fiction is a chapter that examines how the appeals work together in one particular work, the BBC film *Threads*. The final chapter speculates on the possible effect antinuclear fiction may have had on American attitudes toward nuclear weapons during the period from 1945–1990.

While the focus of the book rests firmly on the examination of how fiction as such works as a rhetorical tool in relation to the issue of nuclear weapons, the reader will easily detect a recurring secondary interest. Given the wide range of aesthetic merit in the various works I examine here, I am intrigued by the relationship of the artistic and the rhetorical elements in works of fiction. Considering the widely held critical disdain for overtly didactic works, we may assume that there is a certain inherent tension between artistic effort and rhetorical intent. We may even conclude that works that are most successful rhetorically are doomed to artistic failure.

However, I think the following study may suggest—without attempting to prove systematically—that the relationship between art and rhetoric in a work of fiction may be more complicated. True, in some works, rhetorical elements do seem to ride rough-shod over the artistic, leaving the audience with a disappointing aesthetic experience. Certainly I have encountered more than a few works of antinuclear fiction that fit that description. But I have also found other works—*Dr. Strangelove, Threads, Testament, Rid-dley Walker* to name just a few—that combine art and rhetoric so deftly that the power of each is enhanced.

Whatever success an individual artist may have in combining these elements, however, the effort itself is impressive—and in-teresting in its own right. And when the object of the rhetorical effort is the elimination of the nuclear threat, we may finally conclude that it is important as well.

2

The Dynamic of the Ethical Appeal in Fiction

As I indicated earlier, the ethical appeal stems from the perception the writer gives of his character. Traditional rhetorical theory maintains that the audience is more likely to accept the author's message if he can create a strong positive image of himself. Certainly the 1988 presidential campaign supports the validity of this principle. By the fall of 1987, the campaigns of two candidates for the Democratic nomination—Gary Hart and Joseph Biden—had foundered because of doubts raised about the men's characters. In each case, the candidate protested that the questions raised were irrelevant or inconsequential, but both resigned from the race because concerns about character were obscuring the real issues of the campaign. In other words, the men could not win the voting public's allegiance to their platforms until they had first cleared doubts about their basic personalities. Their resignations, and the reasons given for them, provided tacit agreement with Aristotle's assessment of the vital importance of the ethical appeal: "It is not true, as some writers on the art maintain, that the probity of the speaker contributes nothing to his persuasiveness; on the contrary, we might almost affirm that his character is the most potent of all the means to persuasion."[1]

But what are the components of a positive ethical appeal—the hallmarks of a sterling character? To some extent the answer to this question will vary from age to age and culture to culture, depending on the specific virtues a particular group of people value. Nevertheless, most of us can agree with the three qualities that Aristotle maintained provided a foundation of the ethical appeal: intelligence, character, and good will.[2] The speaker must indicate a sufficient knowledge of the facts at hand and the judgment to make the proper relationships between those facts. He also must convince the audience that he is virtuous enough to relay the facts truthfully and advocate the position that he sincerely feels is best. Finally, he must show that he has the audience's best interests at heart in maintaining his position.

We might recall that, as far as Aristotle was concerned, the ethical appeal depended on the speaker's being able to convince his audience that he possessed these qualities, whether or not he really did. And while other rhetoricians insisted that the truly effective speaker must actually have a sterling character, the success of confidence men the world over suggests that Aristotle was right in maintaining that the *impression* of a positive character is as effective as the positive character itself.

At any rate, whether the ethical appeal is the result of a sincere projection of the writer's character or a skillful manipulation of the audience's perceptions, I cannot stress its importance enough when we are dealing with a subject as difficult and as technically involved as that of nuclear weapons. Because so few people understand the complexities of the subject matter, they find it difficult, if not impossible, to evaluate the reliability of statements about nuclear weapons on the basis of their own knowledge. In a highly specialized society such as ours, it is extremely difficult to have a working knowledge of all the technologies that affect our lives and impossible to know them in detail. By the same token, the vast complexities of international relations in the modern world is beyond the understanding of even some professional diplomats, let alone that of the ordinary citizen. Therefore, someone who wants to make a sincere judgment about the nuclear arms race must find an expert whom he trusts to give him the facts without coloring those facts for personal or professional gain. He must find someone whom he believes to have intelligence, good character, and good will. He must, in short, find someone with a strong positive ethical appeal.

Consequently, if someone writes a book, either fictional or nonfictional, intended to oppose the development and use of nuclear weapons, he must take care that the image he projects will instill confidence in the reader. He will want to indicate that he understands all the aspects of the issue at hand, that he is dealing with those aspects honestly and impartially, and that his purpose is not detrimental to his audience.

Now and then a fortunate writer may not have to work too hard to establish his ethical appeal. His audience may already know and respect him before it even begins to read the particular persuasive text in question. For example, when Bertrand Russell wrote *Has Man a Future?* in 1961, he was an internationally famous mathematician and ethical philosopher, a Nobel Prize winner so committed to his pacifist principles that he had been jailed for them. Although he advocated unpopular positions in the book—the necessity of world government, for example—his reputation alone would have gone a long way toward securing a fair hearing for his opinions.

Such a built-in ethical appeal, however, is not necessarily sufficient to win the complete confidence of the audience. Even though the writer may display certain aspects of a strong ethical appeal, the audience may still have sufficient doubts about some other aspect that they will withhold their confidence in him. In the case of *Has Man a Future?*, the quality that Russell had to take great pains to demonstrate was good will. Because he was writing during the Cold War and because the issue of nuclear weapons involved national security, Russell had to be careful to show that his opposition to them resulted from a genuine impulse to protect the lives of his readers and not from a desire to weaken the free world's defenses. In short, he had to be careful to avert charges that he was a Communist attempting to subvert the freedoms of the United States or a Communist dupe unwittingly aiding in such a subversion.

One way that he chose to accomplish this task was to confront directly actual charges of disloyalty that the United States government had leveled against him. In his discussion of the Pugwash movement—a series of meetings by scientists from both sides of the Iron Curtain to find ways of reducing the danger of nuclear war—he mentioned a Senate Internal Security Committee report branding Western members of the movement, including Russell himself, Communists or Communist sympathizers. To refute the charge he pointed out the committee's lapses from candor in quoting him out of context, in suggesting that senility rather than a changing world situation had led to his evolving attitudes toward nuclear policy, and in implying that Klaus Fuchs and Julius Rosenberg were members of the Pugwash movement. In summary he wrote, "I have seldom come across a piece of propaganda more dishonest than this."[3]

Perhaps more important and more effective than his direct attacks on the committee's own veracity, however, was his appeal to the reader's common sense, an appeal that subtly played upon the reader's own perception of himself. In an attempt to expose the simplistic assumptions of the committee, Russell noted the report's implication "that in any more or less friendly contact between any Communist and any non-Communist, the Communist must be capable of outwitting the Non-communist, however great may be the ability of the latter."[4] In effect he was saying that the Senate committee believed that somehow the Communist is inherently superior to the non-Communist, while Russell obviously felt that the two are at least equal. Since, presumably, the non-Communist reader will want to believe himself better than the Communist, he will be flattered by Russell's implicit compliment and insulted by the committee's implicit insult. As a result, he may feel inclined to give Russell the benefit of the doubt, believing in his good will more than in the committee's.

When the writer is not as well known as Russell, the importance of establishing the ethical appeal within the text is, obviously, more crucial. In addition to making his case, the author must make certain that he is projecting a personality that will appeal to a reader who is totally unfamiliar with him. Moreover, he must do so without distracting from the actual case he is making. He cannot focus on his own personality, at least not for very long, for fear of alienating his audience by appearing more concerned with himself than with his subject. In short, he must communicate a positive character as subtly, or even subliminally, as possible. This sort of subtle communication of personality is made by Freeman Dyson in *Weapons and Hope*.

A biographical note in the book informs us that Dyson is a professor of physics at Princeton who has served as a consultant to the Defense Department and to the Arms Control and Disarmament Agency. In addition, he was written a number of articles for such publications as *The New Yorker* and made numerous speeches about the problems of nuclear arms. While all of this is an impressive record of professional accomplishment, it does pale beside the worldwide celebrity of a Bertrand Russell. Thus, the establishment of Dyson's ethical appeal depends on how he presents himself in this book. He must turn an appealing face to his audience even while he is making his case.

To perform this dual function, Dyson makes frequent and effective use of a combination of cold facts and personal anecdotes. For example, he speaks knowledgeably and lucidly about the various aspects of the arms problem. He devotes whole chapters to types of hardware, the complexities of strategic doctrines, and the history of the arms race. All of this information not only provides the basis for his various arguments but also demonstrates his grasp of the complexity of the problem, thereby establishing his credentials as an authoritative guide to the question at hand. But Dyson wants more. He also wants to show that this expertise stems from personal experience by making a point of the fact that he is himself a scientist and that he has been involved in military matters.

To do so, he uses the anecdote. For example, to demonstrate that the most sophisticated weapon is useless unless it can be deployed in actual combat, he tells us about his experiences during World War II in helping to develop automatic gun-laying turrets for Allied aircraft. Dyson relates that although his scientific team was able to conquer the seemingly impossible task of developing the turret itself, it was unable to develop a system by which the radar could distinguish between enemy planes and friendly ones. The principal importance of the anecdote is to suggest, by analogy, that the MX system is an unfeasible and costly technological boondoggle. In the process of making this point, however, Dyson has communicated relevant facts about himself. He has demonstrated, and not just asserted, his experience and skill in developing military technology. He has also shown that he has the humility and the honesty to admit not only the limitations of military technology in general, but also his own failures as a military technologist. Finally he has revealed an insider's sympathy for the occasional necessity of developing such technology.

Anecdotes are even more valuable to Dyson in establishing his moral integrity. The attitudes that he expresses and the values he seems to support will, of course, give some insight into his moral character. Thus, the very fact that he is concerned about nuclear war and openly expresses revulsion for some of the more inhumane details of strategic theory suggests a strong reverence for life. But his even-handed treatment of the strengths and weaknesses of the two sides of the antinuclear debate and the respect with which he speaks of certain military men throughout the book indicate his refusal to lock himself into a narrow, doctrinaire approach to the issue. He resists the temptation to look for clear villains and simplistic solutions.

Dyson's use of anecdotes allows him to give a direct and vivid impression of this basic sense of morality. Early in the book, he relates that as a young man before World War II he was a strict pacifist but, realizing that pacifism was not always the most appropriate response to aggression, joined the fight against Nazi Germany. Overtly Dyson relates this incident to support his contention that armed defense of one's country is justifiable, and, to the extent that he wishes his reader to share that view, he is inviting us to approve his renunciation of strict pacifist principles. Since the enemy that he chose to fight was one of the most evil in the history of mankind, few of his readers will withhold that approval. Without expressly saying so, however, he is also pointing to two of his admirable qualities: the idealism that led to the pacifism and the flexibility that enabled him to abandon an untenable position. Thus, while apparently doing nothing more than illustrating an abstract point, he is actually giving the reader an insight into his own basic decency and judgment. Later he relates a more recent anecdote demonstrating the fact that he still possesses these characteristics. In 1981 a peace group of which he was a member was debating various antinuclear tactics. While Dyson favored urging the government to adopt a no-first-use policy, the majority voted to support the nuclear freeze movement. Although he felt, and still feels, that the no-first-use policy would have a greater practical effect on reducing the threat of nuclear arms, he supported the majority decision and notes that the freeze movement was a superior device to galvanize public opinion. Once again, Dyson brings up the incident to illustrate the need for politically effective tactics in fighting nuclear weapons. At the same time it demonstrates that he is still idealistic enough to take part in grass roots protest movements, instead of just writing books about his views, and flexible enough to adapt that idealism to practical situations.

Dyson's use of anecdotes presents a potential problem, however, with the question of good will. On several occasions he finds it necessary to refer to his formative years in England, his native country. For example, in discussing the question of fallout shelters, he cites the camaraderie that developed in the London air raid shelters during the Blitz: "Americans can never share the feelings of warmth and friendliness which Europeans of my generation associate with our experiences of shelters in World War II."[5] As we have seen, he writes about his pacifist tendencies when he was in school in England before World War II and about his work with the RAF during that war. The trouble with these anecdotes is that he may begin to sound like a foreigner to an American audience and make it question how sincerely he has its welfare at heart. One need not be a Russian or Chinese Communist to raise the suspicions of an American audience, especially about questions dealing with national security and foreign policy. Any voice that seems to be criticizing from the outside is liable to call forth a degree of xenophobia.

Perhaps to forestall such a reaction, Dyson frequently makes clear his American citizenship. In fact, at the very beginning of the book, he speaks about returning to the United States, his "adopted" country, from a vacation, thereby indicating strongly, but indirectly, that he has *chosen* to live in this country. He repeats this implication at various crucial points throughout the book. Just two paragraphs after the statement about the air raid shelters he speaks of his concern for his new country: "So long as our land is loaded with nuclear weapons, serious shelter-building is ethically unacceptable."[6] Almost immediately after noting a difference between himself and a native American, then, he reasserts his identity as an American citizen and shows his concerns for his new countrymen by speculating about how they might best protect themselves from nuclear weapons.

The effect of these various strategies is to give the reader a positive image of Dyson. He is most of all an intelligent, compassionate man who worries about the nuclear threat but who does not see simple solutions to it. Moreover he is open to arguments from all sources, conservative as well as liberal, the military man as well as the peace worker. The implication is that the arguments and solutions he presents are the considered result of his having sifted through the best of everyone's ideas. Thus, the reader will feel that here is a man whose opinions can be respected, whether they happen to agree with his own or not. As is true in any work, the ethical appeal in *Weapons and Hope* does not necessarily guarantee the reader's acceptance of Dyson's arguments, but it does help insure a fair hearing for those arguments.

The same dynamic holds when fiction is the medium of attempted persuasion. Whether the form is novel, play, or film, audiences will feel more receptive to the work if they are confident that the author is intelligent, virtuous, and sincere. A work, for example, that is an official product of Soviet propaganda sources would obviously lack any real rhetorical appeal for the majority of Americans. Even a work by someone whom the public perceived to be too liberal might suffer an erosion of its rhetorical potential, no matter how sincere and even artistically sound that work might be. If, on the other hand, the audience can see that a work is the product of a thoughtful person who respects the freedom and security of the American people, it is more likely to listen to, and even sympathize with, the author's efforts.

Once again, the creator of a fictional work may have a positive ethical appeal above and beyond the work itself. Such is the case with Pearl S. Buck, whose *Command the Morning* deals with the scientific quest to build the atomic bomb. At the time Buck wrote the novel in 1959, she was a very popular writer widely known for her sensitivity to other cultures and her respect for human life and freedom. In fact, she was the first woman recipient of the Nobel Prize for literature, an award which, for better or worse, frequently elevates a writer to the status of literary sainthood. This reputation no doubt helped her to maintain her audience while she dealt with the still volatile issue of the morality of the use of the atomic bomb against the Japanese.

A number of other writers could also trade on a certain immediate ethical appeal at the time they produced their works. Nevil Shute closed a long career of writing popular novels about serious issues with *On the Beach*. C. P. Snow's *The New Men* was part of the *Strangers and Brothers* series of novels detailing how conflicts between morality and power shape, and sometimes destroy, the human character. Both of these authors could count on large audiences that respected them and relied on their senstivity and insight. By 1964, when *Dr. Strangelove* and *Fail-Safe* were made, Stanley Kubrick and Sidney Lumet enjoyed a similar degree of immediate ethical appeal. Kubrick's antiwar film *Paths of Glory* had paved the way for his popular and critical successes *Spartacus* and *Lolita*. Lumet had made *Twelve Angry Men*, which demonstrated his commitment to social justice, and *Long Day's Journey into Night*, which showed his artistic predilections.

On the whole, however, a film director's name is less recognizable to a wide audience than is a popular novelist's. While the film industry itself largely perceives the director to be ultimately responsible for a film, its actual prior ethical appeal, as far as the public at large is concerned, usually comes from the actors who are cast in the leading roles. The Hollywood star system has been a long-standing admission of the fact that actors develop certain screen images that cause audiences to build up certain expectations of them. While this can sometimes be a source of frustration for the actors themselves, it does often provide an instant attitude toward the characters they play that can be valuable both artistically and rhetorically. For example, the opening shot of Stanley Kramer's film of *On the Beach* is a closeup of Gregory Peck's face. Despite the wide variety of characters he has played, Peck's image tends to be that of the quintessential upright American. Film critic Ephraim Katz, in fact, describes him as "A leading star of Hollywood films whose tall, dark, and handsome figure has projected for three decades of filmgoers moral and physical strength, intelligence, virtue and sincerity."[7] Besides being primary components of Aristotle's definition of the ethical appeal, these qualities are precisely the ones that Peck's character, Commander Dwight Towers, is supposed to possess. Thus, the opening shot of the film automatically disposes the audience to think well of the character and, by extension, the film.

In most cases, however, the creator of a fictional work will have little automatic ethical appeal to rely upon. Novelists like Mordecai Roshwald and Russell Hoban and film makers like Lynne Littman are relatively unknown to the public at large. In these cases the artists, like many of the writers of nonfiction, must create an ethical appeal within their works. Their task in this respect, however, may be somewhat more difficult. The nonfiction writer, given the nature of his medium, can afford to be somewhat more forthcoming in displaying his moral character. Freeman Dyson, as we have seen, can tell anecdotes about himself that reveal aspects of his personality. The fiction writer, however, usually finds it inappropriate to stop in the middle of a novel to talk about himself. How then, does the artist establish an ethical appeal in a work?

The least equivocal way the author can accomplish this task is by supplying his own more or less direct commentary and letting the audience make its own conclusions about his character on the basis of that commentary. When he is writing his work from the third-person point of view, he can comment on the action, evaluate the characters, and make philosophical points that have some relationship to the story that he is unfolding. Even if he lacks the objective voice that a third-person narrator supplies, the author can make his points by placing his commentary in the mouths of characters, including a first person-narrator, whom he has created in his own image. Thus, when General Black denounces the use of computers to order nuclear attacks in *Fail-Safe*, he is actually speaking for Eugene Burdick and Harvey Wheeler, the authors of the novel.

Of course, this technique presents some potential problems for the audience. How does one know whether certain characters are speaking for the author? How does one know, for that matter, that even a third-person narrator is actually identifiable with the author? He may be using an ironic narrator, as Swift does in "A Modest Proposal." To solve this dilemma, the audience must examine the commentary in the light of the whole work. If the action of the piece tends to support the statements of certain characters, we can assume that the opinions of those characters reflect the author's own. Because he can control absolutely the world that he has created, the fiction writer can give a character the force of a prophet simply by causing the action of the novel to support whatever that character says. If the author is at all interested in persuading the reader, he will give this force only to characters with whom he agrees.

Philip Wylie's novel *Triumph* illustrates this point. Written from the third-person omniscient point of view, it describes the destruction of the Northern Hemisphere in a full-scale nuclear war and details the efforts of fifteen Americans to survive in an elaborate fallout shelter. In commenting on this series of events throughout the novel, Wylie leaves little doubt about his political sympathies. For example, when describing the crisis that precipitates the war, he summarizes the history of East-West relations this way: "Threat, counterthreat, compromise, and—usually—some slight retreat of the free world that, as time passed, showed itself to be greater than it had first appeared" (26).[8] The implication of this comment is that American diplomacy since World War II has allowed the Soviets to gain persistent advantage, and we may assume that Wylie would like America's leaders to adopt a more aggressive policy. Moreover, he leaves no doubt about what he sees as the Soviets' ultimate goal: "What, fundamentally, the free-world leaders—military and political—had never understood was that the Russian Communist leaders had always been willing to pay *any* price whatever to conquer the world, so long as some of the Soviet elite survived to be its rulers" (46).

The behavior of Wylie's Soviets indicates that these statements reflect his actual views. His Soviet premier promises the American president that he will not annihilate the free world, but does so only to make the West drop its guard. Even after devastating the North American continent with their first attack, the Soviets set off a number of nuclear mines in the Atlantic ocean to saturate the United States with additional radioactive fallout just when they calculate any survivors of the initial strike would begin to come out of their shelters. Months after the war, the Soviets bombard the United States one more time to make absolutely sure that the population is completely destroyed. While these actions might seem excessively savage to the reader, Wylie explains them as steps in a coldly calculated plan. His Soviets have purposely instigated the war in order to destroy the United States, thereby eliminating any effective opposition to their dreams of world conquest. The fact that this plan calls for the annihilation of over 90 percent of their own citizenry in the inevitable American counterattack does not deter them in the slightest; they have insured ultimate victory by stockpiling people and weapons—including nuclear warheads—under the Ural mountains. Thus, the novel is an illustration of Wylie's own contention that the Soviets will "pay any price whatever" to achieve ultimate victory.

Many, of course, might find this view of the Soviets simplistic— even dangerously so—but it does at least protect Wylie from the charge of being soft on communism. In fact, judging from these attitudes, one could see him fitting comfortably into the extreme right wing of the Republican party. On the positive side, this aspect of his character would give him a high level of ethical appeal among ultra-conservatives—those, for example, who believe the continued survival of the United States depends on our maintaining weapons superiority over the Soviets. While readers from this camp would be suspicious of antinuclear works in general, they might at least be receptive to one written by a man who shares their suspicions of the Soviets. On the negative side, however, these anti-Soviet sentiments might well cause liberal minds to wonder about Wylie and his work. They might dismiss him as a militarist who is actually fueling the arms race with his fears rather than helping to make the world safer from nuclear weapons. They may see him as a spokesman for the old guard, complacent, suspicious of reform, and convinced that civilization is best maintained in a society dominated by capitalism.

Wylie's ethical appeal is not so simple, however. His attitude toward racial and religious bigotry, for example, does not fit the profile of the arch-conservative, especially as that profile would have been constructed in 1963 when the novel was written. While the group of fifteen people whom Wylie preserves from nuclear destruction is headed by a white businessman, the hero is a young Jewish scientist who provides the moral backbone of the novel. The other minority members of the group, two blacks and two orientals, are all very positive characters. Most importantly, Wylie gives both his minority women beauty and dignity and treats sympathetically the attraction of the white men for them. In fact, a reflection on the absurdity of sanctions against interracial relationships leads to an attack on bigotry as an underlying cause of the war: "A dozen branches of science, in thousands of unanswerable tests, had shown no special quality or superiority in black men or white, red, brown, or yellow; Jew or gentile or Moslem or Hindu. But most human beings, and the arrogant white man in particular, had refused to examine the evidence and accept the truth; and in that rejection of known reality they now had lost . . . everything" (189).

This is a surprisingly strong statement, especially when one considers that Wylie is singling out the dominant racial group of his society for special criticism. If his view of Soviet treachery seems to be to the right of Ronald Reagan, his insistence on laying the blame for most of the world's problems at the feet of "the arrogant white man" may strike many as being to the left of most mainstream liberals.

More to the point, Wylie's vivid treatment of the effects of nuclear war suggests that he may have as much aversion for nuclear weapons as he does for the dreaded Soviets themselves. He vividly describes the heat wave that melts the ground, vaporizes buildings, and destroys all life within the immediate radius of ground zero and the shock wave which, farther out, flattens even the strongest structures. He goes on to detail the various horrors that can befall a human being during nuclear warfare: blinding from the flash of the weapon, burning from the after fires, asphyxiation in shelters from which the fires suck all oxygen, and death from radiation poisoning. None of these details of the novel is consistent with an attempt to downplay the danger or destructiveness of nuclear war. On the contrary, it is difficult to see how a person could read them and not develop a disgust for nuclear weapons.

Wylie's ethical appeal, then, is more complex than it might at first appear. Ultimately he seems to be a decent man with a sense of justice and the courage to attack what he sees as the destructive elitism of Western society but who has a profound, even paranoid, conviction of the danger of the Soviet threat. He seems to believe that nuclear weapons will necessarily play a role in world affairs until the nations of the earth find a way to deal justly and peacefully with each other, probably through some form of world government. The fact that this perception of his character contains elements that appeal to both extremes of the political spectrum may help insure that a wide range of audience will trust him enough to read to the end of the work and consider his view seriously.

Wylie is not alone among antinuclear writers in letting his own voice echo so clearly in his work. Burdick and Wheeler open *Fail-Safe* with an author's note describing and decrying the problem that the novel will focus on: the possibility of accidental nuclear war caused by a technological malfunction. And although the remainder of the book, like *Triumph*, is written in the third person, it strongly recalls the tone of that initial statement, thereby reinforcing our initial impression of the authors as thoughtful, concerned men who have a degree of expertise in the field.

We can find an even more direct—and more complex—intrusion of author into work in James Kunetka and Whitley Strieber's novel *Warday*. In this fictional documentary of a future America destroyed by nuclear war, the authors choose themselves to be the main characters, each of whom narrates alternate chapters in the first person. Thus, not only the direct commentary of the narrators, but also the dialogue of the main characters legitimately echo Kunetka and Strieber's own views. What makes this technique so complex, however, is that the characters who narrate the book openly admit that, as a result of the war, their personalities have changed. They have, for example, grown more religious and less materialistic than they were in the early 1980s—the time, in fact, that *Warday* was actually written. In short, we are led to believe that the ethical appeal of the Kunetka and Strieber who narrate the book is, to some extent, distinct from that of the Kunetka and Strieber who are writing the book. On the other hand, we are well aware that the real Kunetka and Strieber have created—or projected—the fictional ones and may actually respect the change in values that they hope the reader will admire. At any rate, this interplay of the authors and their projected selves keeps their own ethical appeal at the forefront of our minds, so that, when they deliver their denunciations of nuclear weapons and their appeals for international human understanding, they can rely on their own direct ethical appeal.

There are, however, certain dangers to a fiction writer's taking such a high profile in his own work. On the one hand—Wylie's hand—he risks allowing his work to become less a fiction—a creation of a credible world inhabited by credible characters—than a thinly disguised diatribe in which marionettes masquerading as people twitch to the writer's obvious agenda. As we shall see in a later chapter, such a work may do more to alienate the reader then to win him over. He will, in Sidney's terms, cease to be delighted when his expectations of fiction are disappointed, and, consequently, be repulsed by the instruction that is so obviously being forced upon him. On the other hand, the more artistic intrusion of the author's ethical appeal that Kunetka and Strieber employ may become distracting and lead away from the point being made. For example, John Fowles's excellent *The French Lieutenant's Woman* uses direct authorial commentary and direct authorial intrusion to explore matters of artistic convention. While such an exploration is at the heart of Fowles's purpose, however, it would be irrelevant to that of many fiction writers. It would certainly distract the reader from an exploration of the issue of nuclear weapons.

Instead the fiction writer will generally remain hidden in his work. Any conception we are to have about him we will have to glean indirectly from it. The choice of subject matter, of course, will provide a major clue to the writer's personality. The very fact that he is so concerned about the dangers of nuclear war will suggest something about his character. And, of course, the same qualities of the text that helped confirm the ethical appeal of the high profile narrator will suggest the nature of the more reticent author's character. Thus, we can gain some insight into a fiction writer's ethical appeal by spotting the inevitable signs of that character in the choices he makes.

In reality, however, the average reader is probably not terribly aware of the author's personality as he is reading the book. Because the writer remains hidden, we are probably more influenced by another source of ethical appeal unique to fiction itself: the ethical appeal of the author's created characters. If the writing is good enough, the characters in the novel will come alive in the reader's imagination and will consequently wield their own ethical appeal—an appeal that may be even more effective than that of the author since the character's personality is more vividly and more constantly present in the reader's .mind. Moreover, the ethical appeal that the author creates for his characters can legitimately differ completely from his own, thus compensating for weaknesses in his personality. When his characters speak, however, they can deliver the thoughts that their creator most firmly believes and wants the world to embrace.

Mordecai Roshwald's novel *Level 7* provides a good illustration of this use of the fictional ethical appeal. The book is narrated by the main character, an army officer identified only as X-127. Thus, all the information we receive, every statement Roshwald wishes to make, will have to be filtered through a created intelligence. Moreover, the character's personality evolves during the book to such an extent that the attitudes he expresses at the end completely contradict those he held at the beginning. Since the author's personality presumably did not experience a similar metamorphosis while he was writing the book, we can be sure that, at points, X-127's thoughts and attitudes must differ from Roshwald's own.

At the beginning of the novel, we learn that X-127 is a push button officer in his country's armed forces. Because not everyone is qualified to be a push button officer, he is proud of his position and even disdainful of his commanding officer: "[H]e was our superior in rank but inferior to us in technical education, in I.Q. and—so we thought—in his indispensability for modern warfare. . . . Our attitude probably resembled that of a bunch of Ivy-league college boys under a veteran sergeant who ruled as a god on the parade ground but with whom they would not have dreamt of associating in private. I wouldn't know for certain because I was never an aristocrat and our instruction bore little resemblance to the old-time training for officers" (6).[9]

Certain crucial aspects of X-127's personality manifest themselves in this passage. He makes a point of the fact that he is a common man, not an aristocrat. On the other hand, he is, and takes great pride in being, a member of an elite group that is instituting a new form of war, and this sense of elitism alienates him from those less gifted—in this case his commanding officer. The reader will eventually realize that Roshwald is planting here the seeds of an interior personality conflict that will afflict X-127 throughout the novel: a sense of commonality—of being a part of humanity—against feelings of elitism and alienation.

X-127's complacence about his position begins to crumble when he is ordered to Level 7, a bunker four thousand feet underground housing the command center for his nation's nuclear arsenal. The security arrangements of Level 7 require that it be a self-sustaining community from which no one is ever allowed to leave. When X-127 realizes that he will never see the sun again, he begins to appreciate what he has taken on in becoming a PBX officer. He must live in an unnatural environment with very little privacy, somehow staving off boredom even though he can never fulfill his function—pushing buttons to unleash his country's nuclear arsenal—unless a faceless, nameless voice over a loudspeaker tells him to. In short, X-127 is fated to live the remainder of his life in the sole company of that elite group he is so proud of, a whole life waiting for the war that only he and his colleagues are able to fight.

Surprisingly, instead of rejoicing in the fact that he will never be bothered again by intellectually and technologically inferior people like his old commanding officer, X-127 initially has mixed feelings about Level 7. On the one hand, he consciously strives to adjust to his new home. He faithfully takes his six-hour tours of duty in front of his push button, waiting to perform his fateful function; he helps a teaching officer to develop a new mythology for Level 7 in which hell is up and heaven down; and, in an extreme effort to find some normality in his new life, he marries a female psychological officer. On the other hand, he finds he can never quite reconcile himself to a perpetual underground existence. He is obsessed with the belief that he can smell the sewage of Level 7 in the air and taste it in the food; he has recurrent dreams in which he witnesses the horrors of nuclear war; and he keeps a diary of his experience in the irrational hope that, even if *he* does not emerge from underground, one day *it* might. In short, he begins to question the basic assumptions of Level 7 and begins to repeat ironically the loudspeaker's contention that Level 7 is the best of all possible worlds.

When fellow push button officer X-117 suffers a nervous breakdown because an attachment to his mother makes his isolation on Level 7 unbearable, X-127 begins to grow conscious of the root of his own conflict. A psychiatrist blames X-117's breakdown on a failure of tests designed to screen out people who were too sensitive and too attached to others to serve effectively on Level 7. Upon hearing this explanation, X-127 begins to question his own character, wondering why *he* is not sensitive enough to have been excluded from Level 7. His pride in being a PBX officer falters now that he realizes that the principal qualification for his position is a cold-hearted alienation from his fellow man, and he begins to envy X-117's attachment to someone other than himself. Ironically, however, even as X-127 is berating himself for his alienation, he is recounting dreams in which he watches in horror while his mother is killed in a nuclear war. It is clear to the reader, although not yet to X-127 himself, that he is much like X-117.

The outbreak of nuclear war finally forces X-127 to confront and resolve his conflicts about his life in general and Level 7 in particular. Realizing that the whole surface of the earth has been destroyed, he must face the fact that now there is definitely no hope of going back to the life he knew before his entombment in Level 7. When X-117 commits suicide out of guilt for his part in the war, X-127 begins to realize the true nature of what he has done and to regret his own participation. And when a leak in the nuclear reactors spreads a plague of fatal radiation poisoning throughout Level 7, he is forced to see that, even by Level 7's very limited standards, his life is a failure: his function was to insure his country's continued existence in the event of nuclear war, but even the small remnant of his countrymen that are cowering in the supposed haven of Level 7 are now condemned to certain death. As a result of the tragedy, however, X-127 is finally able to see Level 7 and its whole philosophy for the sham it is. "Never in human history," he says, "was there anything so grotesque. Two vast countries, the two greatest world powers, reduced in a matter of hours to the status of a few moles, hiding below ground in the constant fear that the next hour will be their last" (135). Now that he has taken part in the destruction of the world and seen that destruction for the terrible tragedy it is, X-127 can deliver Roshwald's attack on nuclear war. Now, instead of writing myths that will support the mission of Level 7, he, like Roshwald himself, writes a symbolic story about the madness of nuclear war.

At the end of the novel, X-127 is the only person left alive on Level 7. Indeed, he is the last person alive on earth. By now he has come to realize that he is not as detached from his fellow man as he had thought: "Even a dying soldier on a battlefield cannot have felt as lonely as I feel . . . I would give anything to have some people around me" (142). Early in the novel he had gloried in his alienation from his fellow man. Later he had questioned the virtue of that alienation. Now, when that alienation has become tangible and irreversible, he realizes that it was illusory. He does need people; he does need to be connected to the human community. But, of course, this realization has come too late. His sense of alienation has allowed him to push the buttons that have destroyed the world, and now there is no human community for him to join. At this crucial point, Roshwald suggests an identification between X-127 and the human race in general. As he begins to succumb to radiation sickness, X-127 writes, "I am dying and humanity dies with me. I am the dying humanity" (142). Roshwald's message is clear: X-127 is everyman, and his struggle to see through the apparent alienation of his life and endure the absurdity of his death is everyone's struggle to maintain his or her humanity in the nuclear world.

Our aesthetic satisfaction with the novel largely depends on our appreciation of the metamorphosis of X-127's character. The spine of the work is the development of his realization of his own nature, and the poignance it imparts stems from the fact that that realization comes too late to prevent humanity's ultimate destruction. In the end, because Roshwald has allowed us to see X-127's character so intimately, we are saddened as much by the individual tragedy of his death as we are by the collective disaster of the destruction of the world. At the same time, because we come to realize that X-127 represents humanity in general, we are able to generalize our vivid emotional reaction to his death to include all humanity, thereby enabling ourselves to appreciate the destruction of the world more fully than we could if we were considering that event in the abstract. Moreover, because X-127 represents all humanity and because we are members of the human race, we may find ourselves developing a sense of identity with the character, experiencing in his death our own potential deaths.

Besides enhancing the artistic effect of the work, however, these elements also help to increase its rhetorical potential. By the end of the book, when Roshwald allows X-127 to deliver his denunciation of nuclear weapons, we may not consciously have a greater sense of the author's character, but we will have a greater appreciation of—and respect for—his hero. Consequently, we will be more inclined to accept X-127's attack against the forces that have destroyed him, especially since our appreciation of the author's artistic purpose shows us that death symbolizes the death of humanity in general. Moreover, our sense of identification with X-127 may help us to see that our passive acceptance of life in the nuclear age is as unnatural and as fatal as X-127's efforts to convince himself that life on Level 7 is the "best of all possible worlds." Then, with Roshwald's hero, we may begin to see that we can insure our survival not by isolating ourselves behind barriers and arming ourselves with weapons of mass destruction, but by accepting the essential unity of all men.

The ability of literature to create characters, then, is a unique and powerful rhetorical tool. At the very least, it can enable an author with a weak ethical appeal to speak through a created personality with a stronger one. At best it can place the personality of the character, and, therefore, his ethical appeal, at the very heart of the artistic experience. If that personality changes as the result of the conflicts that the novel presents him with and if these changes somehow enlighten us, we have an artistic work with a high thematic content. If we feel compelled to change an opinion or take some action on the basis of our experience of the character's transformation, we have a literary and rhetorical artifact.

3
The Cast of Characters

Given the fact that the characters a writer creates are legitimate—and often essential—sources of the ethical appeal in a work of fiction, it should not be surprising that certain kinds of characters recur repeatedly in antinuclear fiction. Surely few would doubt that certain classes of people—by virtue of age, education, profession, etc.—stand a greater chance of winning the trust of a given audience than others. Moreover, the importance we place on the specialist in our time suggests that the area of a person's expertise might affect his ethical appeal, particularly in regard to highly technical subjects like the question of nuclear weapons.

Someone who attempts to use fiction to persuade an audience would, of course, be aware of these facts and would want to exploit them. And since he has the luxury of creating any type of characters he wants, he is able to place them in some category that he feels would especially appeal to the audience he is attempting to persuade.

Given this dynamic, it is unsurprising that one of the most widely used categories of ethical appeal in antinuclear literature is that of the scientist, especially the nuclear scientist. We have already seen at least one example of the scientist's special ethical appeal in Freeman Dyson's 1984 book, *Weapons and Hope*. But Dyson's statement is merely one of the most recent attempts by scientists to engage in the debate over nuclear weapons. Indeed, the voice of the scientist has been raised against the bomb from the beginning of that debate. Before the atomic bomb was dropped on Hiroshima in 1945, many of the scientists who had developed the weapon petitioned President Truman to refrain from using it.[1] After the war the Federation of Atomic Scientists called for international control of nuclear weapons, warning that a world of individual nations all armed with such weapons would soon perish.[2] Albert Einstein and J. Robert Oppenheimer publicly opposed the development of the hydrogen bomb.[3] More recently, organizations like Physicians for Social Responsibility have tried to warn about the medical implictions of nuclear war and nuclear testing.

The basis of the strong ethical appeal of the scientist is twofold. First, the reader feels sure that the scientist knows what he is talking about. Who would know more about what a nuclear weapon does or how it works than the scientists who invented it? And who would know more about the horrifying effects of these weapons on the human body than a physician? This expertise is so important that even writers who are not scientists are careful to display their scientific knowledge about the subject. Such is the case with writers as diverse as Bertrand Russell, Jonathan Schell, and Edward Zuckerman. Nevertheless, the scientist himself speaks most authoritatively to the audience of laymen.

The other factor that increases the ethical appeal of antinuclear scientists is the matter of self-interest. Many scientists have nothing to gain and everything to lose by opposing nuclear weapons. Since the 1940s the weapons industry has been a major source of employment for the scientific community. Not only does the government provide jobs for theoretical scientists who might otherwise be employed as educators at educators' salaries, it also provides enormous amounts of funding for research that private industry could never generate.

Thus, if the continued buildup of nuclear weapons is of immediate value to anyone, nuclear scientists are certainly among the primary beneficiaries. When someone takes an action that will almost certainly have an adverse effect on his professional success, we are more likely to accept his claim that his action stems from a desire to perform some higher good for his society. No doubt this principle was in Dr. Helen Caldicott's mind when she recounted the story of Bill Perry, a scientist at the Lawrence Livermore laboratories who quit his job and began to work for the nuclear freeze after hearing her speak.[4] The fact that the scientist is risking financial ruin to oppose something that his own science has created suggests to us that he has not only the knowledge to speak authoritatively on the issue but also the strength of character to uphold his readers' long-term best interests above his own short-term welfare.

It is, therefore, no accident that nuclear scientists and the moral dilemmas they face play a major role in the literature of the issue. Many of the earliest novels that dealt with the question of the bomb revolve around the historical dilemma of the scientists who developed it. James Hilton's *Never So Strange*, Pearl S. Buck's *Command the Morning*, C. P. Snow's *The New Men*, and Dexter

Masters's *The Accident* all fall into this category. Each explores the relationship between the scientist, his science, morality, and public policy.

Snow, for example, develops his treatment of the nuclear scientist's dilemma in the context of the relationship between two brothers. Martin Eliot is a young physicist involved in the British effort to develop an atomic bomb during World War II, while his older brother, Lewis, is a politician overseeing the project for the government. From the outset, Snow manipulates us into sympathizing with the scientist by introducing him as he is announcing his engagement to a woman who is clearly wrong for him, a fact of which only Lewis and we are aware. The engagement reveals Martin's emotional vulnerability while providing a sympathetic reason for his involvement with the bomb project: he needs to succeed in his career so that he can support his family.

This initial sympathy is important because the attitude that Martin soon begins to display toward his work suggests a detachment from humanity that the average reader may find unattractive and even dangerous. Gladly seizing any opportunity to advance his career, he accepts Lewis's offer of a place on the bomb project, even though he expresses a conviction that if the device works it may well destroy the human race. To be sure, he trusts in the fact that the bomb will not be developed before the war ends, but we have no doubt that his primary interest is not the survival of democracy but the advancement of abstract science. In fact, Snow takes great care to arouse our suspicion of Martin's motives. Reflecting on Martin's participation in a scientific breakthrough, Lewis muses that there are two kinds of scientific experience. After comparing the more noble kind to the mystic's sense of oneness with the universe, he describes Martin's own experience: "Not so free from self, more active: as though, instead of being one with the world, he held the world in the palm of his hand; as though he had, in his moment of insight, seen the trick by which he could toss it about" (50–51).[5] Despite Lewis's avowals that the experience is somehow "pure," his description of it is not likely to attract our sympathy. Inherent in it is the image of the scientist that laymen fear: someone so fascinated by the sheer joy of discovery that he has no regard for what effects his discoveries will have.

So Snow begins his novel by humanizing the basic image of the scientist. He is the detached, and therefore dangerous, person of popular conception, but he is also a loving brother, a touchingly loyal spouse, a devoted father, and a suitably skeptical servant of the government. We are thus encouraged to sympathize with the scientist even while we feel concern about his work. In this way Snow increases our sense of the character's authority by allowing him to help develop the bomb, but preserves his capacity to serve as an effective moral spokesman later in the book.

The level of the moral conflict the scientists in the novel face becomes clear whenever the question of the utilization of the bomb arises. When asked if the government would actually use the bomb, Lewis answers that he finds the idea "almost incredible." Martin replies that he finds it absolutely incredible and goes on to outline the steps he and his colleagues could take to insure that the weapon would never be used. Even so, he is elated when his team manages to build a reactive pile, and he shares his colleagues' joy when the Americans finally do develop the bomb. His justification for this attitude is that someone is bound to find the secret one day, and, if the Allies find it first, he and his colleagues will be able to keep it from being used.

Ultimately, of course, *The New Men*, like most novels dealing with the development of the atomic bomb, points up the impotence of the scientists to control their own creation. It passes into the hands of the military and the government who have few qualms about using it. Having failed to prevent what he has come to see as a misuse of his work, Martin is forced to face the reality of his life: scientific research is not abstract; it has practical, sometimes destructive, results. Following the bombing of Nagasaki, he decides to resign his position with the bomb project and take up a much less prestigious career as a teacher. Ultimately, he reports to Lewis, he can find no compromise: either he accepts the responsibility for the deaths that his work brings about, or he can have nothing to do with developing the weapons. Martin has finally seen that he cannot separate his actions from their consequences. He must accept moral responsibility.

What is the rhetorical effect of this rejection of the bomb by the very people who helped develop it? In one respect, it illustrates the horror that even nuclear scientists historically have felt about the bomb and its effects. It encourages us to think that if they, who know those effects better than anyone, are reluctant to use the bomb, we should be too. And the fact that the scientists in the novels are initially in love with the project increases our sense of their revulsion. They are turning against the practical application of the knowledge they love so much and have struggled so hard to obtain. They are, in effect, sacrificing their lives' work in order to preserve humanity, and that level of sacrifice emphasizes the level of revulsion they feel.

At the same time, the fact that the scientists have created the bomb invests them with a proprietary interest in it. They have given the world a certain knowledge—a certain power, in fact—but have forbidden its use. A reflection on the biblical myth of Adam and Eve and the Tree of Knowledge may help underscore the notion that our violation of this prohibition takes on the nature of a kind of Original Sin of the nuclear age. What right do we have to use the bomb if those who created it have withheld their permission for its use? How can we justify our actions in such a circumstance?

Closely paralleling this use of the scientist as a spokesman against the bomb is the use of the enlightened soldier. In a sense, the soldier's position is similar to that of the scientist in the literature of nuclear war. He also speaks with an authority born of intimacy. While the scientists developed the bomb, the military actually used it against Japan and then insisted that we stockpile the weapon after World War II. The history of the nuclear-arms race is replete with examples of how the military's shortsightedness and lust for power helped increase the numbers and kinds of nuclear weapons in the nation's arsenal. Given this history, we should not wonder that the public image of the military in relation to nuclear weapons is of a group of aggressive and insensitive men who plot cold-blooded strategies for World War III and are all too ready to put those strategies into operation.

Certainly this view of the military prevails in antinuclear works ranging from Ralph E. Lapp's *Kill and Overkill* to Helen Caldicott's *Missile Envy* and Edward Zuckerman's *The Day After World War III*. Unsurprisingly, this attitude appears to a significant degree in antinuclear fiction as well. Such works as *Command the Morning*, *The Accident*, and *The Day the Earth Stood Still* all present military figures whose stern and often thoughtless policies frequently add to the nuclear dilemma. The quintessential portrait of this sort of military type, of course, is found in *Dr. Strangelove* where General Jack D. Ripper initiates a strike against the Soviets because he fears they are fluoridating his water.

Given the pervasiveness of this unflattering view of the military, we may initially be surprised to find how many sympathetic portraits of soldiers can be found in antinuclear fiction. Two of the main characters in *On the Beach*, for example, are naval officers, themselves victims of the war without having taken any real part in it. The hero of Ben Bova's *Millennium* is an Air Force colonel whose sensitivity to human life causes him to commit treason in order to stop a nuclear war. Even the tough-minded, gung ho Air

Force general in *War Games* eventually shows a willingness to listen to reason, withholding a counterstrike when scientists tell him that warnings of a Soviet attack are the result of a technical malfunction.

Because this image of the sensitive, enlightened soldier runs so counter to popular perceptions of the military's attitudes toward nuclear weapons, we may well speculate about its prevalence in antinuclear fiction. Why would an author choose his antinuclear spokesmen from the group of people who would seem least likely to provide such a spokesman? One answer to this question, of course, may be artistic. The very fact that the author chooses the least likely candidate to speak against nuclear war confounds our expectations and provides his work with a degree of complexity. The mystery is always more intriguing if the butler *didn't* do it. A second, perhaps more important, reason for an author's presenting sympathtic military men is that the popular conception of the heartless soldier is not entirely accurate. We have seen that Freeman Dyson draws sensitive portraits of enlightened soldiers in his work. Zuckerman points out that no less a paragon of military correctness than General Douglas MacArthur warned against the horrors of nuclear war.[6] In 1983 a group of former NATO generals wrote *Generals for Peace and Disarmament* to point out that increasing nuclear arsenals actually decreases the security of Western Europe.

Finally, of course, there are compelling rhetorical reasons for putting antinuclear arguments into the mouths of military men. The dynamic of the ethical appeal at work here is similar to that which worked in the case of the scientists. The audience feels that if anyone would support nuclear weapons, a military man would. He, after all, is the professional trained to pursue victory at any cost, dismissing sentimental concerns about individual human life. If he questions the value of nuclear weapons, he presumably does so for strategic reasons, and his objections undercut the rationale for the weapons' existence. We might put up with their horrible potential if they were necessary for the defense of the country, but if even the military questions their usefulness, we might be unwilling to risk total destruction by relying on them.

Such a dynamic is at work in Eugene Burdick and Harvey Wheeler's *Fail-Safe*. The hero of the book is Warren A. Black, an Air Force brigadier general and a member of the Pentagon Alert Group. He is the scion of a wealthy San Francisco family and has inherited an intellectual tradition and an altrusitic conviction that each individual exists primarily to be of service to his society.

Black himself—eschewing the usual family careers in business or politics even though he was intelligent and diligent enough to graduate from an Ivy League school—has brought the tradition with him into the Air Force. Although killing his fellow man troubles him, he sees that it is sometimes necessary to do so. Moreover, he shuns personal glory, remaining intent, instead, on being a capable, reliable officer. Thus, Black presents what we might consider an anomalous image of the military. He *is* a soldier, and he *does* love his service, but he is also a cultivated humanitarian and a self-effacing man of integrity. The reader who expects the soldier to be a mindless militarist will have to reevaluate his attitudes when confronted by Black.

Therefore, when Black expresses doubt about the wisdom of various aspects of the arms race, we are disposed to consider his position seriously. For example, early in the novel we are told that, while he considers the Soviet Union dangerous, he feels that it is not the overwhelming threat that many believe. This conviction undercuts the whole theory of the need for nuclear weapons to keep Soviet conventional forces at bay. Later he off-handedly attacks the philosophy of overkill: "Who needs more muscle now? Neither side. . . . This thing of piling up bombs on bombs and missiles on missiles when we both have a capacity to overkill *after* surviving a first strike is just silly" (146).[7]

Of course, Black also expresses opinions about the central issue of the novel, the possibility of accidental nuclear war. Although he was one of the first Air Force generals to recommend psychological testing for military personnel who would be in a position to command a nuclear strike, he is not convinced that such a system can completely prevent the possibility of some mad general's—or a mad president's—ordering his planes to bomb the Soviet Union. And he is all too well aware of less spectacular forms of human weakness—ranging from fatigue to incompetence—that can lead to the failure of a complicated technological system. Moving beyond the realm of human failure, Black refers to the fact that such intricate systems can never really be fully tested before they are deployed, citing instances in which other kinds of equipment failed in the field. Indeed, he makes the point that, of its very nature, a nuclear force can be thoroughly tested only in the event of all-out war.

Doubtless many of these points are based on actual incidents or studies that Burdick and Wheeler are eager to popularize. But the fact that they associate the statements with a military figure that we have come to care about at once personalizes them and makes them more credible. Because we know the man who delivers these thoughts, we pay more attention to them than we would if they were the pronouncements of an anonymous study. We trust Black to tell us the truth. At the same time, because we know that he is a loyal, competent officer, we have confidence in the military soundness of his opinions.

Black's negative attitudes are not limited to the specifics of the problems of accidental nuclear war, however. He ultimately identifies the irrationality that underlies all aspects of the nuclear arms race. Thinking about the various parties involved in the nuclear arms debate—military men and heads of state, the Left and the Right, hawks and doves, the United States and the Soviet Union—Black concludes that everyone has been overwhelmed by the terms of that debate: "They were caught in a fantastic web of logic and illogic, fact and emotion. No one seemed completely whole. No one could talk complete sense. And everyone was quite sincere" (151). This passage, which anticipates the attitude that Dyson would take two decades later in *Weapons and Hope,* suggests the irrationality, even madness, that the subject of nuclear weapons can generate in otherwise stable, reasonable people.

In the end both Black's negative view of the arms race in general and his specific fears about accidental war are justified. Because a malfunction in a fail-safe box has caused an American plane to bomb Moscow, the president of the United States, to prove that the bombing was an accident, must order Black to bomb New York, Black's home. A technical accident combined with the convoluted antilogic of nuclear weaponry has forced upon Black the ultimate contradiction: to protect his homeland, he must destroy his home; after preparing for a lifetime to kill the enemy if such is his duty, he finds that duty requires him to kill his own family. Burdick and Wheeler have arranged for him to consummate his anomalous function in the novel by becoming both the reluctant perpetrator and submissive victim of nuclear destruction. In doing so, they have increased the strength of his ethical appeal by showing his worth as a prophet: the actions of the book demonstrate that his fears about nuclear war were well-founded. And by placing our ultimate realization of the worth of Black's objections in the same scene in which we most sympathize with him, they give their message its greatest chance of success. Thus, the force of Black's ethical appeal, as it is developed in the book, marshals our sympathies for his, and the authors', arguments against nuclear weapons.

Such positive treatments of the military in antinuclear fiction far outstrip sympathetic portraits of civilians who control nuclear weapons. For example, the leading villain in *Fail-Safe* is a civilian adviser who urges the president and his staff to undertake a preemptive strike against the Soviets. Other works—*Wargames, A Canticle for Leibowitz,* and *Dr. Strangelove,* for example—also present civilian experts who, out of stupidity or blindness or insanity, do more to contribute to the nuclear crisis than to solve it. Politicians do not fare much better. True, the president in *Fail-Safe* is an enlightened, rational man who puts his duty to humanity above considerations of personal or political gain or loss, but more frequently the chiefs of state in antinuclear fiction lack a strong ethical appeal. The president in Ben Bova's *Millennium,* for example, is ineffectual and stupid. After the destruction of the country in *The Day After,* the president delivers a pompous statement assuring his people that the United States will prevail against its enemies. Even in *Riddley Walker,* which is set years after a nuclear holocaust has destroyed civilization on earth, the leader of the atavistic society portrayed in the novel follows a mindless quest to redevelop the "1 big 1" that led to the destruction in the first place.

If heads of state have not, for the most part, been in the forefront of fictional movements to oppose the bomb, however, another type of leader *has* played a consistent role in such opposition—the clergyman. Indeed, the antinuclear stances of fictional men of the cloth have been much more nearly uniform than that of their real-life counterparts. True, clerical opposition to nuclear weapons does trace its roots to the very beginning of the atomic age. After the bombing of Nagasaki, both the Vatican and the Federal Council of Churches of Christ in America questioned the morality of atomic warfare.[8] Continuing this tradition into the present, the Episcopal House of Bishops, in 1982, and the United States Conference of Catholic Bishops, in 1983, each issued pastoral letters calling for eventual global nuclear disarmament. The General Assembly of the United Presbyterian Church in the United States, the United Methodist Council of Bishops, and the National Council of Churches all issued resolutions specifically supporting the nuclear freeze.[9]

But other religious leaders have given tacit, and sometimes explicit, support to the arms race. In the 1950s Pope Pius XII, while condemning the terrible destructive force of the atomic bomb, suggested that its use could be morally justified in extreme situations.[10] More recently, certain ministers in the United States—leaders of the New Right—have taken that attitude several steps further by repeatedly asserting a divine mandate for nuclear superiority. In 1980, for example, the Reverend Jerry Falwell suggested that the United States was failing in its duty to God by falling behind in the nuclear arms race: "Ten years ago, we could have destroyed much of the population of the Soviet Union had we desired to fire our missiles. The sad fact is that today the Soviet Union would kill 135 million to 160 million Americans, and the United States would kill only 3 to 5 percent of the Soviets because of their anti-ballistic missiles and their civil defense."[11]

Religious leaders in antinuclear fiction, however, if not quite unanimous in their opposition to nuclear weapons, at least seem to present an overwhelming consensus. It is difficult, if not impossible, to find a religious figure in these works who joins with the Reverend Falwell in seeking God's blessing for the bomb. In works as varied as *Testament* and *The Day After,* fictional clergymen either attack nuclear weapons directly, or are sympathetic victims of nuclear destruction. In *A Canticle for Leibowitz,* Roman Catholic monks deliver Walter M. Miller's message that knowledge without faith and compassion can lead to destruction: "We all know what *could* happen if there's war. The genetic festering is still with us from the last time Man tried to eradicate himself. Back then . . . [t]hey had not yet seen the madness and the murder and the blotting out of reason. . . . My sons, they cannot do it again. Only a race of madmen could do it again" (255–56).[12] Twenty-five years after the publication of Miller's book, Whitley Strieber and James Kunetka also use a priest to denounce nuclear war: "Modern nuclear war means life being replaced by black, empty space. It means ancient seats of government evaporating in a second. The moral question is almost beyond asking. What are we that we can do this? What is evil, that it can speak with such a voice?" (139).[13]

The ethical appeal of the clergy is not difficult to understand. Clergymen have consistently placed highly in polls measuring which classes of people the public at large respects most. Apparently even in an age when the efficacy of institutionalized religion is questioned, most people are still impressed by those who sincerely dedicate their lives to the service of their God. Moreover, while clergymen are not involved in the development or use of nuclear weapons, they are experts in their own sphere: the ethics of the weapons.

Even the clergyman's image, however, sometimes requires some modification if he is to present a positive ethical appeal to the public at large. A comparison of Abbot Zerchi in *A Canticle for Leibowitz* with Fr. Michael Dougherty in *Warday* illustrates this point. A crucial plot movement in the third part of Miller's novel concerns Abbot Zerchi's attempts to prevent a woman who has been exposed to radiation from seeking euthanasia for herself and her infant daughter. The abbot is here following the dictates of orthodox Roman Catholic doctrine that any taking of innocent human life, for whatever reason, is a serious offense. The denouement of the novel, upholding as it does the primacy of spiritual rule over natural philosophy, makes it clear that the reader is expected to applaud the abbot's stand. Between 1959 and 1984, however, concepts such as euthanasia gained public acceptance to such an extent that many people reading Miller's novel might consider Abbot Zerchi unreasonable, if not heartless, for insisting that the woman accept her suffering. Such a case would certainly be indicated by the way Strieber and Kunetka handle the subject in *Warday*. In this work, the authors interview a doctor who has converted to Catholicism only after the pope relaxed the sanctions against euthanasia. Consequently, their Fr. Dougherty never has to face the conflict between duty and compassion that Abbot Zerchi must struggle with, and he—and the authors—need not risk alienating either the faithful, who might be annoyed by the sight of a priest sinning against his duty, or more secular readers, who might be repulsed by what they perceived as his utter heartlessness. In this way, Strieber and Kunetka emphasize the most positive aspects of the clergyman's ethical appeal without introducing others that might alienate a secular audience.

Traditional rhetorical theory would, no doubt, approve—even applaud—the use of the various classes of ethical appeal we have discussed so far. Scientists, military leaders, and clergymen all seem to have the basic requisites of the ethical appeal: knowledge, virtue, and good will. And even where various of these classes might be presumed to lack some element of these qualities, their creators have been careful to compensate for those deficiencies: Martin ultimtely achieves virtue; Black reveals his intelligence; Fr. Dougherty displays a humanist's view of good will. Other classes of ethical appeal that have been used in antinuclear literature, however, might raise the classical rhetorician's eyebrows a bit.

The use of the special ethical appeal of women in antinuclear fiction, for example, actually violates Aristotle's observations in the *Rhetoric*. Reflecting the views of his times, the great philosopher stumbles a bit in twentieth-century eyes by maintaining that women, like slaves, possess no positive ethical appeal. A look at the literature of nuclear war, however, shows that women, in fact, exercise a significant ethical appeal. One of the strongest voices in the antinuclear movement today, for example, is that of Dr. Helen Caldicott, a pediatrician formerly on the staff of Harvard University Hospital. She has spent several years touring the world speaking against both nuclear weapons and nuclear power, has written two books on the subject, and has contributed to at least two films. In all of this activity, some of her impact is based on her credentials as a physician and a self-made expert on nuclear issues. But a large part of her ethical appeal—and a part that she repeatedly emphasizes—is that of a woman capable of giving birth and traditionally concerned with the nurturing of children.

In *Missile Envy,* she sets out the philosophical background of the special ethical appeal of women, maintaining that there are essential psychological differences between men and women. Men, she claims, are emotionless, excessively logical, and incapable of admitting mistakes. They are competitive and eager to prove their masculinity, frequently through violence. Above all, men are obsessed with their virility and fear that any sign of tenderness may be taken as a sign of impotence. Women, on the other hand, tune in to their feelings, willingly admit mistakes, and listen to their almost unerring intuition. Most of all, the woman is nurturing. Caldicott claims that, like the male's instinct for violence, this nurturing quality is inborn. It helps women rise above competitive urges and find ways to compromise. She compares relations between world powers to marriage and points out that it is always the woman who makes the initiative that resolves marital conflict. The nurturing aspect of a woman, of course, gives her a great concern about children and, therefore, about future generations in general. Because of this concern, she detests war.

Whatever one thinks of this conception of the differences between male and female traits—and men may, perhaps, be forgiven for not thinking much of it—the concept that women have a unique ethical appeal in relation to questions of war and peace has been strong in both fictional and nonfictional works about nuclear arms. Pearl S. Buck used the women's perspective in *Command the Morning* by placing a denunciation of the mind set that developed the bomb into the mouth of the technically ignorant but deeply feeling wife of the project head. In *Fail-Safe* General Black's wife interrupts a theoretical discussion of nuclear strategy to deliver a humanist view of the issue: "Man has calculated himself into so specialized a braininess that he has gone beyond reality. And he cannot tap the truth of his viscera because that, for the specialist, is the ultimate sin. . . . Your concern, the two of you, is to make sure that you die intellectually correct. But my problem is more primitive. I only want to make sure that when it comes and my boys are dying that I am there to ease their last pain with morphine" (95–96).

It may say something about the general awareness of this aspect of ethical appeal that, when the novel was made into a film in 1964, this speech was eliminated and the character of Black's wife was reduced to the level of a supportive "little woman" whose principal dramatic function was to be present in New York City when duty forced Black to drop a bomb on it. I suspect that twenty years later a director with Sidney Lumet's progressive sensibilities would have been more concerned with bringing out Mrs. Black's ethical appeal.

The development of the general public's consciousness of the woman's viewpoint during the last twenty years may be inferred from the fact that in 1984 a woman, Lynne Littman, was able to make a major film about nuclear war from a woman's viewpoint. *Testament* details the death of Hamlin, California from the radioactive fallout of a nuclear strike in San Francisco. Although the central character is a housewife named Carol Wetherly whose struggle to keep her family together as her world crumbles illustrates the nurturing impulse of women, the film maintains its artistic integrity by making its points subtly. No one delivers passionate speeches about the differences in viewpoint between the women who suffer the effects of the war and the men who, presumably, planned and carried it out. Instead the nurturing of family life is built into the film's point of view and structure.

By opening with various scenes detailing the beginning of a typical day in the Wetherlys' lives, Littman establishes the difference between the mother's orientation and the father's. We see the mother attending to domestic details—picking clothes off the floor, fixing breakfast and making sure that her daughter eats it, getting her youngest dressed, even taking out the garbage. While these actions are the sort that many feminists might decry for perpetuating false stereotypes of the woman's role, they are necessary for the preservation of orderly family life, and it is the preservation of the family that lies at the heart of the particularly feminine ethical appeal. While the mother is performing her role as the foundation of the family's smooth existence, her husband, Tom, is pursuing his own early morning routine. He takes his usual bicycle ride with his older son, challenging him to race up a steep hill. While he is supportive of the boy's efforts, he does betray an underlying sense of competitiveness combined with a slight insensitivity that seems to fit Caldicott's assertions about the differences between men and women.

The next section of the film, a discussion between Carol and her husband in bed that night, reinforces this perception. At first Tom wants to sleep, but Carol wants to talk about what to get the oldest son for his birthday. He complains that the birthday is two months away and there is no reason to worry about it now. But she is insistent and eventually reveals her real concern: the son is getting older and will eventually have to face the draft. Once again, Tom complains that she is being impractical, pointing out that the son will not be draft age for five years. The scene is written and played semicomically, the humor stemming from the husband's reasonable contention that it is too soon to worry about his thirteen-year-old son's being hurt in a war. The underlying conflict of the scene, however, illustrates Caldicott's view of the opposition between men and women. The father appeals to logic to quiet the mother's fears—fears that arise from her instinctive, nurturing concern for her child. Having answered those fears to his own satisfaction, he then ignores the fact that his arguments have not really quieted those emotions but simply transformed the concern into anger. Moreover, subsequent scenes vitiate the smug ridicule that grows from the father's logic. War is closer to his family than he could possibly imagine. It is, in fact, only a day away. Thus, the film justifies the woman's irrational emotional concern for her son's safety and undercuts the father's "reasonable" complacence.

The balance of *Testament* repeatedly renders the horrors of nuclear war in domestic terms. For example, we witness the explosions themselves totally from the perspective of the Wetherlys' living room. The scene begins with the children watching television while the mother takes care of family business. Suddenly a news bulletin about hostilities between the United States and the Soviet Union interrupts the program. When, in turn, static interrupts this bulletin, the mother, perhaps responding immediately to some intuitive sense of danger to her loved ones, gathers the children in the center of the room, clutching them to herself in an attempt to cover them with her own body. Later we see the first evidence of the deadly fallout in a fine dust covering the family's breakfast dishes. Even the breakdown of social order is rendered in domestic terms. A neighbor boy breaks into the Wetherlys' home to steal food—more of an issue for mothers to handle over the back fence than a crime that demands the attention of the National Guard.

Indeed, the whole dramatic structure of the film depends on this emphasis on domestic matters, following, as it does, the gradual disintegration of the family as one member after another dies. First Tom is presumed killed at work in San Francisco. Then,

in a series of low-key scenes we watch the deaths of the youngest
son and the daughter. Intercut with these moments—actually
punctuating the deaths—are home movie views of the family's last
celebration together—Tom's birthday. The film climaxes when
Carol decides to commit suicide with her son and an orphaned
neighbor boy. In preparation, she straightens up her house, ar-
ranging knickknacks on her youngest son's dresser, closing the lid
on her daughter's piano, touching her husband's pictures. All of
these actions remind her, and us, of the family unit that is now all
but destroyed. Then she takes the children to the garage, closes
the door, and starts the car. Before she can lose consciousness,
however, she relents. She finds she cannot destroy what is left of
the family. She must cling to what remains, even though logic
tells her that the situation is hopeless. Her decision, as Caldicott
might point out, is typically a woman's response. Ultimately she
cannot destroy the family because it is against her very nature to
do so. Instead she decides to celebrate the son's birthday—a
festival of life—with the meager food they have available. When
the son asks what to wish for, the mother delivers her final
speech: "That we remember it all, the good and the awful. The
way we finally lived. That we never gave up. That we will last to be
here to deserve the children."[14]

These lines echo an incident that takes place shortly after the
attack. At the end of a performance of "The Pied Piper of Hamlin"
given by the local school children, the mayor of the fairy-tale
Hamlin mourns the loss of his children and curses his own stupidity for causing that loss. The parallel between the leaders of the
legendary town and the leaders of the countries of the real world
is obvious. The suggestion that the leaders of the world have
betrayed the children, and, by implication, future generations by
allowing a nuclear war is a central part of the woman's ethical
appeal. Caldicott would say that the leaders have destroyed the
very people they were supposed to nurture. Littman underscores
this concept with a subplot about a young couple whose baby dies
of radiation poisoning. Significantly, the first sign the couple has
of the baby's illness is her refusal to nurse because her mother's
milk is contaminated. Here we have the quintessential metaphor
for a woman's view of the horror of nuclear war—it makes her
unable to fulfill her primary biological function: to give and to
nurture life.

The concept that the world does not deserve its children suggests another kind of ethical appeal—that of children. Of course,
depictions of youthful victims to arouse emotions of pity are

legion. We think of children as innocents, especially in the ways of international politics. Of all the potential victims of the horrors of war, children are the most poignant. So, as we shall see later, writers have paraded suffering children through both the nonfictional and the fictional literature of nuclear war in an attempt to arouse their audiences' emotions. It is also possible, however, to find instances when children are permitted to act not so much as passive victims but as persuasive spokesmen in their own right.

Even Aristotle in the *Rhetoric* recognized the potency of the ethical appeal of the child—or, to be more precise, the male youth. He points out that the young man is more idealistic than his elders because experience has not yet taught him the necessity of tempering virtue with prudence. Consequently, the youth is predisposed to act on principle. At the same time, however, Aristotle warned of the weaknesses of the youth's ethical appeal. While idealistic, the youth is also prone to rashness. Moreover, the youth's idealism is offset by a tendency to be overwhelmed by passions, particularly anger and lust.

Valuing the balance that the tempering of idealism with prudence gives, Aristotle placed the ethical appeal of mature man much higher than that of the youth. But social critics of our own day do not always share his view. Especially in the last fifteen to twenty years, the advantages of the unique attributes of youth have, for some people, all but supplanted the role of experience in persuasive appeal. The passionate idealism that Aristotle grants to youth often projects a more attractive sense of sincerity than does the tendency toward compromise that maturity frequently urges. In fact, at various points in recent history, compromise has been seen as the product of failed idealism or outright corruption in "mature" people. Even the more passionate nature of youth can be an advantage rather than a liability. Recent popular culture has frequently portrayed youthful anger as a legitimate reaction against the evil of the adult world. Increased freedom of sexual expression among the young is often seen as a sign of vitality and an instinct to create that the older generation has lost.

We are dealing here with a Wordsworthian view that begins with the assumption that children are naturally good and naturally wise. Indeed, in this view, children are morally and intellectually superior to adults. It is an attitude that flavors some of Caldicott's comments in *Missile Envy:* "Children also seem to have an intuitive sixth sense about truth which adults usually lack. . . . Children are so honest and straightforward that their comments are often disarming to adults, who prefer to dismiss their profound truth as childish thinking and therefore not to be taken seriously."[15] While many parents and teachers might wish to qualify this view somewhat, we do have to admit that it has achieved widespread popularity. For example, many believe that the Vietnam War was hastened to its close by the protests of idealistic young students. More recently, a twelve-year-old schoolgirl, the late Samantha Smith, became an international celebrity by writing to Soviet Premier Yuri Andropov—and, subsequently, visiting the Soviet Union—to plead for world peace.

Antinuclear fiction, of course, has not ignored the power of this appeal. Riddley Walker, who rejects the pursuit of nuclear technology in Russel Hoban's novel, is a twelve-year-old making the transition into adulthood but without quite losing the ideals of youth. *Warday* includes a touching chapter in which children writing about spring naively attack the destructiveness of nuclear war. The most effective chapters of Tim O'Brien's novel *The Nuclear Age* depict the hero's youthful revulsion toward the concept of nuclear weapons in the 1950s. The 1987 film *Amazing Grace and Chuck* deals with a schoolboy who protests nuclear weapons by refusing to participate in sports.

But no work has brought the ethical appeal of the youth to a wider audience than John Badham's *Wargames*. The film is an adventure depicting the efforts of two high school students to save the world from nuclear destruction threatened by an out-of-control computer. Even though the pair have some share in perpetrating the crisis by breaking into the Defense Department's computers to play war games, their youth enables them to respond to the crisis more sensitively and pragmatically than their elders.

In the early part of the film, Badham takes time to establish the superiority of the two students to the adult world that surrounds them. To this end, we learn that, although David Lightman seems to be a poor student in school, he is a computer genius when left to his own devices. Moreover, his abilities at the computer terminal enable him to outsmart the adult world and reverse the consequences of his academic deficiencies: he breaks into the school's computers and changes his grades. At home his fad-oriented mother and ineffectual father play out comic scenes, while he sits in his room showing his girlfriend Jennifer that, when he is at his keyboard, he has the world, literally, at his fingertips. This superiority of the youth to the adult achieves its apotheosis when David succeeds in bypassing all of the elaborate security measures that are designed to prevent anyone from tampering with the WOPR

(War Operations Planned Response) computer which controls the country's nuclear capacity.

The use of the ethical appeal of the child in the film comes most obviously into play after the defense computer goes out of control and David and Jennifer attempt to enlist the aid of a scientist named Falken who originally programmed it. Falken, however, has grown fatalistic about mankind's ability to stave off its self-destructive tendencies. He explains to the two teenagers that man, like the dinosaur, has outlived his usefulness and is ready for extinction: "And when we go, nature will start again—with the bees, probably. Nature knows when to give up, David. . . . Extinction is part of the natural order."[16] The boy's response to Falken's suave, cosmic argument is an instinctive affirmation of life: "If we're extinguished there's nothing natural about that. It's just stupid." Though his lines lack the eloquence of the scientist's speech, they reflect two valid points. One is that while the dinosaurs became extinct through natural forces outside themselves, the extinction of man in a nuclear war would be the result of man's own choices. He would become the first species to cause his own destruction. Stemming from this point is the second: since nuclear extinction would be the result of man's own actions, it can be judged as any of his other actions can be. As interested parties, most viewers of the film would probably agree with the boy that such an extinction would, indeed, be stupid.

More importantly, the children are perceptive enough to see through Falken's philosophical arguments to the real reason he is unwilling to help them save the world. Their research into the computer's origins has informed them that Falken's wife and son Joshua were killed in an automobile accident shortly before Falken gave up government research. Jennifer, after listening to Falken's lecture on human extinction, points out that, at seventeen, she is too young to die and suggests that he would help if his son were alive. David, picking up on this theme, delivers youth's age-old rebuke to the adult world: "You don't care about death because you're already dead. I know a lot about you. I know you weren't always like this. What was the last thing you cared about?" This complaint is, of course, the classic one leveled by vibrant, idealistic youth against the cynical, despairing older generation. Significantly, it is this rebuke that seems to change Falken's mind. These two children have forced him to remember the hopes and ideals of his youth—hopes and ideals that he had embodied in his son—and this memory convinces him to help the students ward off nuclear destruction. Later, in a final vindication of the youth's superiority to the adult, David, with Falken's blessing, proves himself more adept than the civilian analyst by teaching the computer that nuclear war is unwinnable before it can launch an attack against the Soviet Union.

The climax of this film brings to the fore another type of ethical appeal that classical rhetorical theory could not possibly have taken into account: that of the computer. It may seem odd to think that a piece of hardware could have an ethical appeal. After all, ethical appeal is supposed to be based on personality and character. Machines, properly speaking, have neither. But, as Aristotle pointed out, actuality is not as important as perception in determining ethical appeal. Because people generally perceive the computer to be an almost limitless thinking machine, they tend to confer on it many of the qualities of a thinking being, including character and personality. In fact, the computer's ability to perform certain functions much more quickly and accurately than a human being may cause many people to think of them as superior beings.

Of course, one might argue that even if they are seen as superior beings, their appeal tends to be more negative than positive. Whenever someone receives a bill that doesn't seem quite right, he immediately blames the computer for making a mistake. More often than not, the human being who issued the bill is only too happy to confirm that suspicion. The computer has become the unseen and defenseless scapegoat for all the bureaucratic problems of modern man. We reason that it is a machine, observe how often our other machines break down, and conclude that it, too, breaks down, probably more often than it should. Popular culture has confirmed this impression and played on the fears it arouses. *Fail-Safe* and *Wargames* are both nightmare tales of what could happen if too many computers had too much control over our nuclear forces.

There is, however, another side to man's relationships with his thinking machines. He may complain about them; he may question their accuracy; he may deride what he perceives as their undependability—but he has learned to rely upon them. If a mistake appears on his bank statement, he may immediately assume that the computer has erred (again), but just as immediately he takes out his pocket calculator to check his own arithmetic. As often as not, he discovers, with no special surprise, that he, and not the computer, has committed the error. The frenzy for buying desktop microcomputers for various domestic purposes ranging from balancing the family's budget to scheduling the family's activities suggests that we trust computers much more than we like to admit. Even the die-hard humanist has discovered the advantages that word processing can provide. The simple fact is that, say what we might, on some deep level the human being does trust the computer in certain areas as much as—or more than—he trusts himself.

An instructive perspective on the changing ethical appeal of the computer can be gained by comparing differing treatments of the most famous of fictional computers, the HAL 9000 from Stanley Kubrick's 1968 film, *2001, A Space Odyssey* and Peter Hyams's 1984 sequel *2010*. HAL is, for all practical purposes, as human as any character in either film. He speaks with a distinctly human voice; he engages in meaningful dialogues with the other members of the cast; and he even has a rudimentary personality with an apparent capacity for emotion. But his capabilities far surpass those of actual human beings. He is supposedly incapable of error, which makes him the perfect being to control the various functions of the spaceship Discovery. As frequently happens in films pitting man against his machines, however, the HAL of *2001* eventually becomes a threat. After making a mistake about the status of a piece of equipment, he realizes that his human companions have begun to lose confidence in him. To maintain his primacy, he tries, in a very human fashion, to kill the crew. It is only by luck and cunning that the last surviving crew member is able to lobotomize the machine and regain control of the ship. The message is ominously clear: man stands in danger of becoming subject to his superhuman machines, which, when they inevitably break down, will pose a possibly uncontrollable danger to the human race.

In 1984 director Peter Hyams made a sequel to *2001* in which a team from Earth reboards the spacecraft Discovery to find out what went wrong with the mission. HAL's creator, Dr. Chandra, revives the computer's higher memory functions, and we learn that its behavior was the result of a neurotic episode triggered by an inability to lie to the astronauts, as mission control had commanded it to do. Thus, not only is HAL's reputation restored in the second film, but it is actually enhanced. We learn that HAL is, in fact, morally superior to his human counterparts: a man can lie, but HAL cannot. And to emphasize HAL's heroic character, Hyams has him sacrifice himself at the end of the film in order to save the human astronauts. Combined with Chandra's contention that a computer is just a silicon-based life form as opposed to the carbon-based forms that created it, these events reflect a powerful positive ethical appeal for the computer.

What we see in these two films, then, is an evolution of people's attitudes toward computers from deep-seated fear to confidence and even awe. Of course, the films themselves simply reflect, with some exaggeration, the general attitudes of society. We *do* place great confidence in computers, and writers and filmmakers can exploit this confidence as they once exploited our fears. Since we have come to recognize the computer's superiority to us in certain respects, the skillful artist can increase the force of his message by placing it in the circuits of a superhuman, but benign thinking machine. Certainly such a process is at work in *Wargames*.

At the beginning of the film, Badham presents the WOPR computer as the usual impersonal bank of blinking lights. Its caretaker explains that the machine plays war games twenty-four hours a day, experimenting with various scenarios for nuclear war in order to point out flaws in strategy. He tells us that the machine's unique talent is an ability to evaluate its own mistakes and learn from them. At this point in the film, the computer has no observable personality, although the caretaker *does* affectionately refer to it as "he," and the camera movements along its surface sometimes seem designed to suggest the movements of a caged animal—or at least a caged intelligence—pacing the confines of its box.

Only when David and Jennifer contact the computer does it begin to take on the trappings of personality. First, the boy discovers that the secret password that will allow him to circumvent the security devices built into the computer is *Joshua*, the name of the scientist's dead son. The students even begin to call the machine Joshua, thus giving it the status of the professor's surrogate son. This suggestion of incarnation is enhanced when the boy attaches a voice synthesizer to the computer, allowing it to "talk" in a high-pitched, slightly mechanical voice like some cartoon character. This quality goes a long way toward making the computer sympathetic, as does the fact that when the boy suggests that they play "Global Thermonuclear War," Joshua seems reluctant, suggesting a game of chess instead; not only is he a lovable buddy and a faithful son, he is basically nonviolent and uninterested in mankind's hostility. Later, when the computer is about to cause the destruction of the world, we may advert to this scene and remember that he is just a dutiful servant who has been programmed to do humanity's dirty work.

At the climax of the film, Joshua has taken complete control of U.S. nuclear forces and is preparing to launch an attack against the Soviet Union. Mankind's sole hope of survival lies in teaching him that nuclear war is futile before he is able to launch one. David is able to accomplish this task by forcing the computer to play tic tac toe—a game that cannot be won. As Joshua goes through game after game without finding a winner, he comes to understand the analogy between the game and nuclear war. In the several seconds left before he discovers the codes that will launch the missiles, he tests what seems to be every conceivable scenario for nuclear war, each one having the same negative outcome. We see the various scenarios flashing on the plotting board—dotted lights tracing paths of missile trajectories punctuated by large flashes indicating explosions. After each scenario, a message flashes "Winner: None." The tempo increases as the computer plays more and more games faster and faster. He discovers the final missile launch code at precisely the same moment he learns his lesson. Instead of launching a strike, he says, "Strange game, Professor Falken. The only winning move is not to play." Significantly, this is the first time the computer speaks over the voice synthesizer in this scene. Presumably no one would have thought to hook up the device during the crisis, so Badham is cheating a bit in order to increase the sense of the computer's humanity when it is announcing the theme of the film.

In doing so, the computer really has only repeated what the scientist has already said, that nuclear war cannot be won and that limited nuclear war is impossible. When Falken first meets the students, he attacks the military's perceptions of nuclear war: "There's no way to win. The game itself is pointless. But back at the war room they believe you can win a nuclear war. That there can be acceptable losses." In delivering this speech, Falken has undercut the reason for the existence of nuclear weapons and, essentially, delivered the main message of *Wargames*. One might argue that the film would be as effective if, having allowed Falken to make this statement where he does—about three-quarters of the way through the film—Badham had permitted the computer to launch its attack, thus proving the professor's point more vividly.

A number of arguments could be made against this strategy, including the fact that the resulting film would have depressed and repulsed the teenaged audience it was intended for. The more important argument, however, is that this scenario would deprive the film of its most potent spokesman—Joshua himself. The simple fact is that when the professor claims that nuclear war is unwinnable, we may tend to trust him because he is an expert. But we know that he is also a fallible human being. He might be overlooking some small possibility of victory. When Joshua tells us that nuclear war is unwinnable, however, we believe him absolutely. He is a computer. He is a thinking machine. He is the first cousin to our department store's computers, our bank's computers, our hospital's computers. Moreover, we know that Joshua has considered all the evidence. We have just seen him examine all the possibilities of nuclear war exhaustively. Consequently, we can be absolutely certain that no options will lead to victory in nuclear war. We subconsciously fall back on our trust that these machines can, in fact, consider such possibilities much more quickly, much more completely, and much more reliably than a human being. For these reasons, Badham gives Joshua the final words: "The only winning move is not to play."

Of course, not all of the heroes and heroines of antinuclear fiction fall into one of the categories we have discussed here. It is true, however, that these are the dominant recurrent classes of characters that have helped provide the ethical appeal in antinuclear fiction during the past forty years. In fact, one is hard pressed to find a work that does not rely on at least one of these categories of ethical appeal. Given the rhetorical artist's desire to do everything in his power to insure the success of his message, we may conclude that these categories of characters are the ones judged most likely to gain the confidence of the audience, at least in regard to the subject of nuclear weapons. We may also note that each of these categories emphasizes a different aspect of the overall components of the ethical appeal. For example, the strength of the scientist's or soldier's ethical appeal rests in his knowledge of nuclear weapons and their use. Virtue and idealism, on the other hand, are more important to the ethical appeal of the clergyman and the youth. Good will, the passionate desire to insure the continuation of the human race, emerges as the primary quality of the woman's ethical appeal.

In any case, the attention that artists pay to their selection of characters is a tribute to the continuing importance of the ethical appeal in antinuclear fiction. As Aristotle pointed out, the ethical appeal is often powerful enough to persuade an audience in and of itself. Even when it does not, however, its function is still vital in that it provides the foundation on which the substance of the rhetorical act—the rational case—frequently depends.

4

The Rational Appeal in Fiction

To examine the dynamic of the rational appeal in fiction, it is helpful to recall the two primary tools of logic: deduction and induction. In deduction we employ the syllogism—beginning with some general principle, applying it to some individual instance, and finally making some conclusion about the specific instance on the basis of the general principle. The classic example of such logical movements is the categorical syllogism about Socrates and mortality:

> All men are mortal.
> Socrates is a man.
> Therefore, Socrates is mortal.

When we reason inductively, we observe a number of specific instances in which the same things happen under the same conditions over and over again. After we have observed enough of these individual instances, we feel confident in making the generalization that, under the same circumstances, whatever happened in the individual instances will always happen.

The dynamic of the rational appeal in rhetoric parallels the workings of logic in that it employs deduction and induction. But because rhetoric deals with probabilities rather than absolutes, the rules for validity in rhetorical induction and deduction are not as stringent as they are in scientific reasoning. So, instead of the strict syllogism of logic, rhetoric employs a looser form of deductive statement that Aristotle called the enthymeme, and in place of the strict induction, it employs the example.

In *Aristotle on Political Reasoning*, Larry Arnhart points out that the premises of the enthymeme are derived not from scientifically verifiable principles but from the common sense opinions of ordinary people.[1] He notes, however, that, although such opinions are only probably true—or true only most of the time—Aristotle does not consider a reliance on them irrational: "The 'reputable opinions' (*endoxa*) on any particular subject are usually confused and apparently contradictory, but Aristotle assumes that in most cases they manifest at least a partial grasp of the truth and, therefore, that any serious inquiry into moral or political subjects must start from them."[2] The reason the enthymeme must start with common opinion—and therefore produce only a partial or probable grasp of the truth—is that it deals with human action and, as Arnhart notes, "in reasoning about human action, probable knowledge is the most that one should expect."[3]

We might be able to appreciate this point better if we look at a particular example. George Kennan has argued against U.S. deployment of tactical nuclear weapons in western Europe. His arguments—what Aristotle would call his enthymemes—stem from the premise that the Soviet Union does not necessarily desire to overrun the region.[4] United States strategy for the past forty years, however, has rested on the premises that the Soviets *do* wish to invade the area and that only nuclear forces could stop them if they did. No one, not even the experts involved, can be absolutely certain which of these premises is correct, but policymakers must decide which is more probable when recommending strategy.

A second quality that Aristotle ascribes to the enthymeme is that it must be readily accessible to an unsophisticated audience who may grow impatient with the painstaking, step-by-step reasoning of the strict logical syllogism. Therefore, the statement of the enthymeme need not be as formally complete as that of the syllogism. Aristotle specifically advises the rhetorician to streamline his enthymeme in two ways: "[Y]ou must not begin the chain of reasoning too far back, or its length will render the argument obscure; and you must not put in every single link or the statement of what is obvious will render it prolix."[5] It is important to remember, however, that, although the statement of the enthymeme is usually incomplete, the reasoning behind it must be sound.

For example, Edward Zuckerman recounts an exchange between nuclear scientist Philip Morrison and a senator in a committee hearing a few months after the bombing of Hiroshima. The senator kept asking Morrison how a man might protect himself from radiation at the site of an atomic blast, and Morrison kept answering that no such protection was possible. When the senator kept bringing up the fact that a lead-lined tank had approached the Trinity test site, "Morrison finally caught on that the senator was from a state where one important industry was the mining of lead. Morrison allowed then that a man could be protected from a bomb's radiation if he wore a fifty-ton lead suit, and the questioning was allowed to get back on course."[6] Clearly, it was unnecessary for Morrison to develop the entire line of argument establishing that, since such a suit would crush a man, there was no feasible and effective means of protecting an individual from the radioactivity of a nuclear explosion.

While the example corresponds to induction in logical argumentation, it does not function in exactly the same way. True induction establishes the validity of a generalization by an appeal to a repeated pattern of specific observations. The rhetorical use of example draws parallels between two individual instances, using the more familiar to explain the less familiar. Thus, a speaker might cite the similarities between the buildup of nuclear weapons in our time and the buildup of conventional weapons before World War I to suggest that the current worldwide nuclear arsenal increases the possibility of war. The inductive quality of the example arises when a speaker or writer compiles a sufficient number of individual examples to suggest the likelihood of some general principle. In the case we are dealing with here, a number of examples of arms buildups which led to war would increase the audience's conviction that arms races generally lead to war.

Obviously, like the enthymeme, the rhetorical example need not meet the same stringent standards for validity that a logical induction would. In order to make a valid scientific induction, one must find a statistically significant number of identical instances without finding any contradictory instances. Rhetorical induction, on the other hand, need not be based on as many individual observations. In fact, Arnhart maintains that the general principle could proceed from one example if it is striking enough: "While induction reasons from all the particulars to a generalization, example reasons from only one or several well-known particulars to a generalization and then immediately applies the generalization to another particular that is less well known."[7] We can see this principle at work in Edward Zuckerman's *The Day after World War III*. Proponents of weapons systems frequently assure the public that the dangers of nuclear war are minimal because only the president can order a nuclear strike and, under the current strategy of mutual assured destruction, only a madman *would* order such a strike. Zuckerman points out, however, that in 1974, when President Nixon was on the verge of resignation and some suspected his mental stability, "Secretary of Defense James Schlesinger deferred all trips and ordered the armed forces to accept no commands from the White House without his concurrence."[8] With this single example, Zuckerman goes a long way toward establishing a rhetorical generalization that the United States' nuclear capacity could fall into the hands of a disturbed man.

One could, of course, expect to find heavy use of the rational appeal in nonfictional rhetorical works. We may initially be surprised, however, to find how extensively the two strategies of rhetorical argument, the enthymeme and the example, enter into the fiction of nuclear war. We tend to think of fiction as a representation of imaginary actions that exist in their own self-contained world. We do not normally expect the author to stop in the middle of relating a story to build a logical argument. And yet, if the action of a novel, play, or film revolves around some controversial issue, the author will find it possible, even necessary, to include in his fictional action a representation of the controversial aspects of the issue, including the arguments that people advance to support their various positions. In this way, a work dealing with the nuclear-weapons controversy will quite naturally reproduce the sorts of arguments a nonfictional work about the issue would set forth.

For example, Dore Schary's play *The Highest Tree* concerns a physicist's rejection of his government's nuclear policy. At the climax of the play, the scientist, Aaron Cornish, explains his position in an exchange with his superior, John Devereaux:

> *Devereaux. In these times there are things we must accept. We must learn, as the saying goes, "to live with it."*
> *Aaron. Yes, if we grow old, or bald, or become sick, or suffer defeat. But if we can effect any change, then it's a sin to "live with it." . . .*
> *Devereaux. Last night, I asked you what you proposed. You said you could propose nothing. Have you suddenly found an answer?*
> *Aaron. I only know your policy won't work, Devereaux. The policy of defending a nation with a plan for mass extermination is suicide—also immoral— also there is no chance for delayed admission of error.[9]*

This dialogue encapsulates a wide range of arguments in the nuclear debate. Devereaux is the apologist for the government's strategy of mutual assured destruction. Given the fact that the Soviets have nuclear weapons, the only thing the United States can do is to keep up with, if not ahead of, its rival. Consequently, the defense establishment must continue the development and testing of nuclear weapons. His position is that, essentially, our country has no choice in the matter. When Aaron counters that man *does* have a choice, he is asserting the idea that, because man has developed the weapons, he can control them. As an attempt to refute this notion, Devereaux challenges him to suggest a workable way out of the nuclear dilemma. Instead of making such a suggestion, Aaron attempts to undercut Devereaux's position by citing the three most popular arguments against mutual assured destruction. If each side has the capacity and the will to destroy the other in the event of nuclear war, any government's use of the weapons is suicidal. The fact that casualties in such a war would include countless noncombatants violates widely held criteria for conducting a moral defence of a country. Finally, because mutual assured destruction works only if a full retaliatory response to an initial strike is automatic, no one will be able to prevent the retaliation even if the first strike is accidental.

In a few short lines of dialogue, Schary has carried on, in brief form, part of one of the principal debates of the nuclear age. He has not developed that debate in all its detail, as someone interested in a strict logical argument would feel compelled to do, but he has, instead, presented it in the form of an enthymeme, leaving his audience to fill in the details of the arguments.

Even the enthymeme, of course, must be buttressed with facts that support the premises on which it is based. Once again, however, these facts need not give the kind of absolute proof to a premise that empiricism might demand. Instead they will establish a reasonable probability that will solicit the audience's support. In nonfiction, this step presents the author with no dilemma. He will simply state his facts as necessary to support his argument. Jonathan Schell, in *The Fate of the Earth,* for example, simply quotes statistics to support his contention that the world would be made uninhabitable by nuclear war. The fiction writer, however, must produce enough facts to make his argument convincing, but not to the extent that he harms the artistic effect of the work. If the presentation of facts supersedes the creation of an illusion of reality, the artistic foundation of the work may be eroded.

The writer can use two strategies to insert factual information into his work. He can simply make the narrator introduce facts as they are needed, or he can have the characters recite those facts as part of their dialogue. In the first instance, he must be careful not to let his novel degenerate into a contrived fact book, as Philip Wylie's *Triumph* so often does. In the second instance, he must make the exposition flow naturally, or at least as naturally as exposition normally flows.

Fortunately for the rhetorical fiction writer, the recitation of facts is as much a part of life as is debate. So an accurate imitation of reality will naturally include the citing of facts by characters. The potential problem is that, in a sincere effort to convey the truth about an issue as serious as nuclear war, the author will want to convey the facts as accurately as possible. In real life, however, people often speak with great conviction about things they are actually unsure of. They even lie to advance their own interests. An absolutely accurate imitation of reality would reflect these human tendencies. Therefore, the writer must balance his desire to convey the truth against his desire for artistic integrity, keeping in mind that if an ethically appealing character in a work says something about nuclear weapons, millions in the audience will believe him.

The degree of effectiveness with which the two methods of exposition can be used is exemplified by Stanley Kubrick's *Dr. Strangelove*. The film is designed to illuminate a number of aspects of the nuclear-arms debate: the suicidal nature of the strategy of mutual assured destruction, the possibility that human failure could lead to nuclear war, the danger of man's being over-whelmed by his nuclear technology, and the absurdity of civil defense efforts, to name a few. Consequently, Kubrick is required to explain the crucial details of a number of aspects of the nuclear-arms predicament. Clearly, he runs the risk of letting his film bog down in a swamp of exposition. When he was preparing the film, however, he recognized that one effective way around that danger would be to use humor. Originally *Dr. Strangelove*, which is based on a serious novel by Peter George, was supposed to be a drama. But Kubrick soon concluded that it would work better as a satire: "The only way to tell the story was as a black comedy, or, better, a nightmare comedy, where the things that make you laugh are really the heart of the paradoxical postures that make a nuclear war possible."[10] These "paradoxical postures" are, at least in part, the very things that will require exposition. Thus, by deciding to make his film a satire, Kubrick insured that the exposition, instead of detracting from the entertainment the film has to offer, would be at the very heart of it.

Dr. Strangelove opens with an example of direct exposition. Over the image of some mountain peaks rising above a cloud bank, a deep-voiced narrator tells in somberly suggestive tones about a secret base that the Soviets have built in a remote, fog shrouded area. The tone and style of the narration reminds us of a typical 1950s B picture and could be the prologue to anything from a paranoid political melodrama to an outlandish science fiction thriller. But Kubrick then goes into a credit sequence that shows a B-52 being refueled by a tanker aircraft while a sentimental rendering of "Try a Little Tenderness" plays on the sound track. The humorous incongruity of music and image is reinforced by the titles themselves, which are printed to suggest skywriting but are proportioned so that, for example, the *A* in "A Stanley Kubrick Production" towers above all the other words in the phrase. While this lettering may be meant to suggest the insane lack of perspective in the nuclear world, its most immediate effect is to amuse the audience and, therefore, to tell them that the film is a comedy. This revelation sets an immediate attitude toward the narrator we have just heard. It throws him into sharp relief; it conditions us to think of him as a dolt who doesn't realize that he is taking part in a satire. Therefore, we tend to ridicule both him and his narration.

Having established his narrator as an oaf, Kubrick uses him to add satiric interest to some necessary exposition about the failsafe system in which B-52 bombers carrying fifty-megaton nuclear payloads patrol the skies twenty-four hours a day just two hours' flying time from their Soviet targets. Because the action of the film will revolve around one of these planes, Kubrick needs to give us some of the details about what it does and how it operates. But the audience, now aware of the narrator's comic naivete, will have the pleasure of laughing at his absurdity even while it is absorbing the terrifying facts he presents.

Kubrick also embeds exposition in the character's speeches, doing so quite naturally and comically. For example, he must explain how an Air Force general was able to launch a strike single-handedly, given the fact that the president is the only official supposed to be able to do so. He gives the crucial lines to Buck Turgidsen in response to the president's outraged demand for an explanation of the command mechanism that allowed General Ripper to assume presidential authority:

> Turgidsen. Well, perhaps you're forgetting the provisions of Plan R, sir.
> President. Plan R?
> Turgidsen. Plan R is an emergency war plan, in which a lower echelon commander may order nuclear retaliation after a sneak attack if the normal chain of command has been disrupted. You approved it sir. You must remember. Surely you must recall, sir, when Senator Buford made that big hassle about our deterrent lacking credibility.[11]

In reality, there *are* provisions for delegating the authority to order retaliation in the case of the president's death during nuclear war, so the information we are receiving here not only provides a crucial justification of the plot but also points up a valid danger of the United States' nuclear retaliatory capacity.[12] The problem with this exposition, however, is that Turgidsen is explaining these facts to the president, who should be aware of them. In a less comic film the more astute members of the audience might recognize this fact and immediately realize that they, and not the president, were the ones being given the information. Kubrick, however, uses this aspect of exposition to his advantage. The confusion that Peter Sellers as President Merkin Muffley registers in his words and actions indicates that, although he approved of the legislation creating Plan R, he has been unaware of its full implications. He *does* need to have the situation explained to him. Thus, for all of Muffley's intellectual mien and authoritative manner, he has, in effect, ceded control of the weapons to military "experts" like General Jack D. Ripper, who has lost his mind and ordered the strike, and General Buck Turgidsen, who recommends that the president take advantage of the situation to destroy the Soviets. Therefore, the necessity of the exposition provides Kubrick with an opportunity to point out that the whole question of nuclear weapons has gotten beyond the civilian authority's understanding and control. And George C. Scott's delivery—a parody of an insurance adjuster explaining difficult clauses in a policy to a claimant—provides the humor that keeps the audience entertained even while the point is being made.

In many ways the use of the example as a form of rhetorical argument in fiction seems more natural than the use of the enthymeme. When an author wishes to provide an invented example, he simply creates a plot that will illustrate whatever point he wants to make. If he wants to attack the strategy of Mutual Assured Destruction, his plot will provide an example of the failure of the balance of terror—as *Fail-Safe* and *Dr. Strangelove* do. Aristotle himself advocates the advantages of fiction to a rhetorical argument based on example. He points out that examples could be either historical or invented and suggests that the invented examples are superior because they can be tailored to the situation being discussed.[13]

To be effective, however, even a fictional example must be plausible. In the 1950s, a spate of science fiction films used the popular fear of radiation to stimulate their audiences. One device was to suggest that radiation from nuclear weapons could cause organisms to change their size radically. Consequently, films showed people shrinking to the size of microbes and insects growing to the size of elephants. A classic example of this genre is *Them!* in which a strain of giant ants—mutants spawned by radiation at the original Trinity test site—invade Los Angeles. While the film shares the crude charm of the best of the science fiction films of the 1950s, its premise is patently absurd: there is no evidence to suggest that radiation would actually change the size of any creature so radically, and studies show that the insect is one of the species that best resist the effects of radiation. Even this fantastic example, however, can take on persuasive force if the audience accepts the giant ants as merely symbolic representations of the magnitude of the unknown problems man unleashed when he entered the nuclear age.

More plausible fictional examples of the effects of radiation are the menagerie of mutants that parade through postapocalyptic novels and films. In *A Canticle for Leibowitz*, characters with spotted face, horns, two heads, and so forth make appearances without unduly shocking the other people in the book. In *Riddley Walker* the "Eusa folk" lack eyes, noses, or ears. Because these mutations, although bizarre, are less extreme than giant insects, we may find them more plausible. Interestingly, however, they may be no more accurate. We know, of course, of instances of children being born handicapped in some way because chemical pollution or excess radiation in their mothers' environments caused genetic damage, but whether or not the level of radiation in a full-scale nuclear war would lead to mutations of the magnitude portrayed in these works is by no means certain. Strieber and Kunetka confront this question in *Warday*. After discussing rumors about dramatic forms of mutation—giant man-eating bats, monstrous children who claw their way out of their mothers' wombs, etc.—they admit that they have found no proof of such mutations. They do, however, find less spectacular but more pathetic forms: children born with decreased mental capacity or without limbs. Since these forms of genetic mutations are more in keeping with known cases of such deformities, they may be more plausible and, therefore, provide a stronger argument.

Interestingly, as Aristotle pointed out in the *Poetics*, an action may be plausible without being possible. In *On the Beach*, Shute suggests that human life could be destroyed if the United States and the Soviet Union fought each other using hydrogen bombs sheathed in cobalt. Shute postulates that the fallout produced by such bombs would remains lethally radioactive for five years after the initial explosions, during which time it could be carried by winds all over the globe. This scenario seemed plausible and was certainly terrifying. There is evidence to suggest that the novel, and the film that was subsequently made from it did have an effect on people's attitudes toward nuclear weapons. But the viability of Shute's projection is actually problematical. It is technically feasible to sheathe hydrogen bombs in cobalt, thereby increasing the length of time their fallout would remain radioactive, but Dyson asserts that, wind patterns being what they are, the fallout would not spread to the Southern Hemisphere quickly enough to destroy all life on earth.[14] He goes on to point out that the fallout that did come down would fall in patches, allowing people to escape death by fleeing to shelters.

Despite this crucial lapse, however, the novel is persuasive for two reasons, First, it is plausible. Someone not trained in the complexities of meteorological phenomena could well accept the scenario Shute presents. Helen Caldicott, for example, traces her opposition to nuclear arms to her reading of the novel while she was in medical school during the 1950s. Second, Shute's story does render in simplified, and therefore readily understandable, terms the concept that man does in fact possess the capacity to destroy life on the planet. Granted, the pattern of bombing in an actual war would probably limit the immediate effects of the weapons to areas in the United States, Western Europe, China, and the Soviet Union, but the only factor limiting the bombing to those areas is the drift of current strategic planning. The delivery systems now is use *could* carry nuclear destruction to virtually any place on the globe.

Moreover, as Jonathan Schell points out in *The Fate of the Earth*, even the experts still do not know what the full effects of a widespread use of nuclear weapons would be. In attempting to determine how the destruction of life in the Northern Hemisphere would affect the whole ecosystem of the Earth, he himself suggests that it might damage that system beyond repair. In the early 1980s, a number of scientists concerned about the ecological effects of nuclear war embarked on a study which ultimately suggested that the firestorms generated by nuclear attacks on cities would throw up a cloud of smoke and dust thick enough to block out the sun and cause a so-called "nuclear winter," which would destroy crops and produce a worldwide famine.[15] In 1986 a Defense Department report confirmed the general validity of this theory.[16] Thus, even if the Southern Hemisphere did not perish along with the Northern as a result of the direct effects of nuclear weapons, it might well perish as the result of indirect effects, thereby substantiating the essential theme of Shute's novel: that man has the power to commit species suicide and must confront that power before it destroys him.

We have examined the two types of rhetorical argument in fiction separately. It is, however, possible to find both enthymeme and example in the same work. An author may portray a debate about a certain problem and then create an actual instance of the problem in the work. Naturally, the way the author handles the instance will tend to support the position of one side of the debate. Throughout *Fail-Safe*, for example, characters argue various aspects of nuclear war, including the possibility that the various machines that control the weapons could trigger an unintentional nuclear strike. A number of characters, including the hero, assert that such an accident is possible. Others, most notably the civilian analyst, discount the possibility. Even while this debate is being carried on, however, a component in one of the machines is malfunctioning, causing just the sort of unauthorized strike that the characters have been debating. If the audience finds the example presented in the novel plausible, they will support that side of the debate which says that accidental war through technical malfunction is possible. Thus Burdick and Wheeler present us with the enthymeme that argues the danger of accidental war and a fictional example that supports that enthymeme. We might say that they have presented the reader with a self-verifying argument against nuclear weapons.

While meeting these rhetorical challenges, however, the writer must be careful not to neglect the artistic concerns of the work. In using the enthymeme, he must be able to create a scene that will plausibly introduce a debate without destroying a sense of verisimilitude. In using the example the writer must be able to manipulate the action of the story to support his point without making that action seem contrived. There are, of course, great dangers in attempting these processes. The author may find himself facing a conflict between artistic and rhetorical demands. Too frequently in this conflict, the rhetorical demands win out, and the work moves in the direction of crude didacticism. This fact probably accounts for the generally poor critical reputation that manifestly rhetorical fiction suffers.

In fact, there are many examples of antinuclear fiction that are inferior because of their failure to balance adequately the two demands. In *Triumph* Philip Wylie frequently halts the development of his story in order to lecture his reader about some fact of nuclear weapons that he wants to publicize, frequently emphasizing his purpose by saying, or having a character say, that these facts are obvious to anyone who cares to look for them. At such moments, the reader has little choice but to advert to the fact that the novel exists largely to popularize this knowledge rather than to provide a stimulating artistic experience. Moreover, Wylie's need to present an example of the potential destructive power of nuclear weapons prompts him to develop his plot in a patently implausible manner: his Soviets are incredibly, even suicidally, savage and the American President is fatally naive. Most crucially, the climax of the novel, in which a remnant of American submarines obliterates deadly Soviet bases, works artistically only at the expense of Wylie's antinuclear message. While his theme seems to be that only universal brotherhood will solve the nuclear crisis, his climax forces his reader to support unquestioningly the total annihilation of the remaining Soviet people.

A less striking, if more famous, example of the failure of a work to balance the rhetorical and artistic demands is the film *The Day After*. While it received a great deal of popular acclaim when it was first telecast on ABC in the fall of 1983, many critics have attacked it for a lack of artistic impact. Moreover, a poll taken shortly after the film was shown indicates that it seemed not to have had a major impact on popular opinions about nuclear weapons.[17] To a large segment of the population, then, the film apparently was not the artistic and rhetorical triumph that its publicity may have claimed.

In an attempt to show us the effects of nuclear war on a typical American city, the film presents examples of the major components of such a war. First, it shows how a nuclear war might begin: a buildup of tension in Western Europe leads to an invasion of West Germany by Soviet conventional forces that provokes nuclear retaliation by the West. The film proceeds to demonstrate the effects the initial explosions would have at several points various distances from ground zero. After the blasts we see examples of how people succumb to secondary effects of the explosions: radiation sickness, disease, and starvation. The presentation is plausible throughout.

The problem with *The Day After*, however, is that, in order to avoid destroying the dramatic flow of the film, director Nicholas Meyer has left the details of his examples unclear. Although the initial appearance of each location is accompanied by a title giving its position in relation to Lawrence, Kansas, the titles appear too quickly for us to orient ourselves. Moreover, when the blasts do come, we must determine where they occurred in relation to Lawrence in order to calculate where the location we are observing is in relation to the blasts. And because the film cuts so quickly from place to place, it is not always clear just which location is being shown at any given moment. While these factors may communicate the chaotic nature of nuclear war, they tend to vitiate the director's attempts to inform us of the direct effects of nuclear explosions.

At other points, Meyer's determination not to force awkward exposition on the audience leaves important rhetorical points totally unexplained. For example, some time after the blasts—we don't know precisely how long—a character emerges from his shelter wearing dark glasses. Evidently the glasses are an allusion to the theory that ozone depletion in the wake of large-scale nuclear explosions could increase to dangerous levels the amount of ultraviolet radiation reaching the earth. Unfortunately, no reference is made in the film to this theory, and the viewer who is not familiar with the more arcane speculation about nuclear war may miss the point completely. Since one of the purposes of the film is to persuade by informing, this omission is puzzling. Most important of all is the fact that, since the film clings determinedly to the unity of place, we are given no real idea of the scope of the destruction. Granted, we are told that the strike was a full-scale one, and characters speculate about the destruction elsewhere, but we are given no visual verification of this destruction.

At the same time, rhetorical claims help to undercut the artistic effort. Because Meyer wants to show the effects of nuclear war on ordinary people like us, none of the characters in the film has any say in whether or not these weapons will be used. Therefore, Meyer cuts himself off from one major source of potential dramatic conflict. And since no one in a targeted area can take any effective action to save himself, the film realistically eschews any portrayal of heroic action among those who happen to be at Ground Zero when the explosions come. While this choice keeps faith with the film's serious intent. it provides a number of characters with nothing to do but scream a little before being incinerated. Much of the latter part of the film shows people dying of radiation poisoning, but, since there is nothing they can do about their problem, this situation also lacks drama. Again and again, Meyer's commitment to showing ordinary, unheroic people as victims of nuclear holocaust eliminates potential sources of drama. Even given this commitment, however, he could have fallen back on one dramatic situation: the choices a person makes when faced with the inevitability of his own death. We have already seen that *Testament* uses this kind of dramatic device to good effect. Here again, however, the rhetorical mission of *The Day After* hampers its artistic potential. Because Meyer wants to show the effects of nuclear war on a cross section of people, he must keep cutting from one character to another in the large cast, never concentrating on one long enough to develop any real psychological depth.

The demands of the rational appeal in rhetorical fiction do not necessarily have to compromise the artistic strength of a work, however. In fact, the rational appeal can contribute to the artistic effect in various ways. For example, the necessity of establishing a self-verifying argument will influence the writer's manipulation of events in the novel. Thus, he will be assured of a work that will have a coherent structure, and structure is an important artistic consideration. On another level, the rhetorical novelist will necessarily produce a work with some strong thematic content. If we feel an affinity with that thematic content—if we can recognize the relevance of what the author is saying to our own lives—we may react even more strongly to the experience offered in the novel than we otherwise would. Of course, in either case the author must manipulate his elements with skill, but the same can be said of an author who has no rhetorical ambitions.

Russell Hoban's novel *Riddley Walker* illustrates how elements of rhetorical argument may be skillfully used to increase the effect of an artistic experience. On its most basic level, *Riddley Walker* is a coming-of-age novel. During the course of the book, Riddley innocently becomes a pawn in a local leader's power play and learns through his experiences that mankind possesses an ineradicable capacity for destruction. In order to make this point about human nature, Hoban calls upon a standard premise of the nuclear-weapons debate.

At the beginning of the novel Hoban plunges his reader into a harsh, primitive world in which boys become men at the age of twelve and anyone who lives to thirty is considered old. In this world, villagers hunt and kill boars with wooden spears and always travel in groups for fear of being ripped apart by packs of wild dogs. In many respects the world may strike the reader as a medieval one, an impression that is reinforced by the style of the book. Narrated by Riddley himself, it begins with the line, "On my naming day when I come 12 I gone front spear and kilt a wild boar he parbly been the las wyld pig on the Bundel Downs any how there hadnt ben none for a long time befor him nor I aint looking to see none agen."[18] The strangeness of the diction and the spelling here suggest an earlier, developmental stage of English before usage was standardized.

Gradually, however, Hoban gives us clues that the world we are dealing with lies somewhere in the future. Telling a folk story, Riddley makes dark references to something called Bad Time, which seems to be the dividing line between the present and "time back way, way back." He goes on to describe this earlier time: "They had machines et numbers up. They fed them numbers and they fractiont out the Power of things. They had the Nos. of the rain bow and the Power of the air all workit out with counting which is how they got boats in the air and pictures on the wind" (19). Obviously Riddley is referring to computers, airplanes, television, and other modern inventions, and we are probably not too surprised when we gradually learn that the world has been plunged into its primitive state by a nuclear war. Thus the basic situation of the book, in attempting to demonstrate how terrible life would be after a nuclear war, provides a type of antinuclear argument by example.

The real significance of Hoban's novel as an antinuclear work, however, lies in the fact that it exemplifies a theory that nuclear weapons are an ineradicable force in our world. Hoban structures the story around this point. Early in the novel we learn that, although the society in general opposes progress, Abel Goodparley, one of the leaders, is obsessed with regaining the glory of "time back, way, way back." Most of all he covets the most powerful manifestation of the "clevverness" of the ancients: "the 1 Big 1," which, we realize, is a nuclear capacity. The portrait of the technological world that Goodparley draws is so seductive that Riddley is drawn into his quest. Of course, we, knowing the technology required to build a nuclear weapon, tend to dismiss their quest as a pathetic yearning for the unattainable. And seeing, as we do, what nuclear weapons have done to the world, we are probably happy that this yearning will remain unfulfilled.

This quest, however, does comprise the plot of the novel, providing Hoban with the structure he needs to develop Riddley's understanding of the nature of man. Shortly after we learn of Goodparley's ambitions, Riddley flees his community following a dispute with a powerful man. After his flight, he meets a mutant boy-man who calls himself Lissener. This character is one of the "Eusa folk," who claim to have preserved the knowledge of the 1 Big 1 through the centuries. Riddley joins him, and they find a bag of "yellerboy stoan," which Lissener maintains is one of the ingredients of the 1 Big 1. Eventually Goodparley tracks them down and brings Riddley and the yellerboy stoan to an old man named Granser. It is at this point that we learn that Goodparley's quest is not so ridiculous as it might originally have seemed.

After admitting that "There won't be no 1 Big 1 for us Abel we aint got the clevverness for it," Granser says that they do have the capacity to reproduce the 1 Littl 1, the precursor of the 1 Big 1. He has already assembled the first two ingredients for the 1 Littl 1— "Saul and Peter" and "chard coal"—and has been waiting only for "the yellerboy stoan." By this point in the novel we have become so accustomed to Hoban's use of diction that we readily recognize the three ingredients as saltpeter, charcoal, and sulfur—the components of gunpowder. And our conclusion is confirmed shortly when Granser blows himself up in an effort to apply "the knowing what ben kep safe right the way from time back way back" (189).

As we shall see in the next chapter, the underlying philosophical point being made here has been a staple of the debate over nuclear weapons for more than thirty years. Since the power of the atom is a constant principle of physics, man's capacity for nuclear weapons can never really be eradicated; even if we could succeed in ridding the world of these weapons, they could always be redeveloped since the secret of how they are made is a constant that can either be preserved or rediscovered. Of course, Hoban makes this point indirectly by substituting gunpowder for nuclear weapons, but the connection made throughout the novel between the 1 Littl 1, gunpowder, and the 1 Big 1, nuclear weapons, is a clear indication that, as Granser says, we are witnessing the first step in a long line of technological developments that will lead to the reinvention of nuclear weapons. Moreover, by making his antinuclear point in this indirect way, Hoban increases the reader's sense of horror.

Throughout the novel the characters have concentrated so exclusively on developing the 1 Big 1 that we are distracted from less grandiose endeavors that might actually be within their reach, and Hoban's use of unusual diction enables him to conceal the fact that they are gathering the components of gunpowder. Consequently, the feasibility of their developing a destructive property takes us more or less by surprise, and their success in developing that property shocks us more than it would have if we, and they, had known all along what they were doing.

This specific point about the persistence of nuclear weapons, however, is part of a larger point about the persistence of evil in human nature. At one point Riddley watches a Punch and Judy puppet show in which a character named Mr. Drop John is responsible for bringing nuclear weapons to the world. Mr. Drop John is described as having a "red face and little poynty beard and the horns and all" (137). Clearly, this character is a representation of Satan, and the fact that he gives nuclear weapons to man highlights their essential evil. At other places we are told that the 1 Big 1 is the result of the ripping apart of "the Littl Shyning Man Addom" who is found in the "Hart of the Wud." Here again, Hoban is using his unusual diction and spelling to make a point. The splitting of the Little Shyning Man named Addom is, of course, a reference to the splitting of the atom. However, the spelling of Addom reminds us of Adam and calls to mind the biblical myth of the fall of man. Theologically this myth explains man's inborn susceptibility to evil. Thus, Hoban seems to be connecting nuclear weapons with the most basic weaknesses of man. The concept of Hart of the Wud supports this idea. In the Eusa story, which provides a mythological account of the destruction of the world by nuclear weapons, the Littl Shyning Man is found between the horns of a stag that wanders through the woods. As Riddley points out, however, "There is the hart of the wood meaning the veryes deep of it" (2). In this meaning, the spelling might more properly be rendered *heart of the would*—the depth of man's desire. Thus, nuclear weapons would arise out of the essential nature of man—out of that basic destructive capacity that is part of man's fallen nature. Given this concept and given the idea that the technology of nuclear weapons is a constant of nature, the fact that man will redevelop these weapons becomes inevitable, and the actual redevelopment of gunpowder as a step toward the reinvention of nuclear weapons verifies this concept of human nature.

It is in realizing this fact of human nature that Riddley comes of age. He now knows that the same "clevverness" that put boats in the sky and pictures on the wind also split the Littl Shyning Man and plunged the world into the state that has caused him to mourn, "O what we ben! And what we come to!" (100). Knowing that the key to a permanent improvement in mankind's condition does not rest solely on technological developments but on the ability of man to confront and control his darker side, he decides to travel the countryside presenting his own Punch and Judy show, one that warns audiences of their destructive capacities. Thus, besides providing an antinuclear warning itself, Hoban's novel directly asserts the validity of rhetorical fiction.

The introduction of rhetorical concerns into a work of fiction, then, can either add to or detract from the total artistic effect of the work. The factor that determines whether the effect will be advantageous or deleterious is the skill of the artist, and not the nature of the message. A Kubrick, a Hoban, a Roshwald can integrate the rhetorical concerns with the artistic purpose so skillfully that each takes force from the other. In doing so, such authors have provided artistic highlights in the history of antinuclear fiction.

5

The Nuclear Debate in Fiction

The combination of entheymeme and example has enabled fiction to follow the major movements of the nuclear-weapons debate from the initial controversy over the use of the bomb in 1945 to the arguments over Reagan's Strategic Defense Initiative in the 1980s. In doing so, fiction has helped to make that debate more accessible to millions of people who might have ignored its presentation in other media.

The first fictional treatments of the debate over nuclear weapons were necessarily retrospective ones because the opening arguments were withheld from the general public for national security reasons. Immediately after the development of the atomic bomb, the U.S government had to decide what to do with it. The military recommended that it be dropped on Japan to end the war quickly and forestall an invasion of the Japanese mainland that would cost an estimated five hundred thousand to one million American casualties.[1] Many of the scientists who had developed the bomb, however, opposed its use. A group of Manhattan project scientists known as the Committee of Social and Political Implications had already issued a report stating that a surprise use of the bomb would hurt the United States' reputation and could make future control of the weapon impossible. Instead, the report suggested, the bomb should be demonstrated on some uninhabited island in the hope that it would intimidate the enemy into surrender.[2] Later, physicist Leo Szilard sent a petition signed by sixty-nine scientists to President Truman urging that the bomb not be used.[3] Victory in the debate, as we know, went to the military. On 6 August 1945, an American B-17 dropped the bomb on Hiroshima. On August 9 a second bomb was dropped on Nagasaki.

The American public first learned of the existence of nuclear weapons in the news reports of these bombings. Although most people did not understand the nature of the weapons, they probably agreed with President Truman's statements justifying the use of the bomb as a means of shortening the war. As we have already seen, however, there were some dissenting voices. Many scientists continued to denounce the use of the bomb and to warn of its threat to the future of civilization. A number of religious leaders either questioned or condemned the use of the bomb and urged the president to halt its production.[4] Publications like the *New York Times* and the *Saturday Review of Literature* published editorials condemning the bombings.[5] The initial public debate over the bomb, then, concerned the morality of the attacks on Hiroshima and Nagasaki. Since these actions were *fait accompli,* however, the question soon became the morality of nuclear weapons in general.

This question soon found its way into fiction. As early as 1947 the popular English novelist James Hilton wrote *Nothing So Strange,* a novel dramatizing the disillusionment of those scientists who became convinced of the immorality of the bomb. At one point in the novel, a scientist likens the bomb to the Nazi death camps and suggests that the United States and its Allies have lost their moral superiority in using it. While Pearl S. Buck's *Command the Morning* presents a slightly more sympathetic view of the bomb's use by emphasizing the argument that it was necessary to end the war quickly, she does allow her hero scientist to level some harsh criticism: "I'm sick. I'm really sick. I still say we had to do it. But I want to get out of the whole damned business. . . . What else could I have done? But I yield to this extent— I ought not to have let myself be put in that position. The glory of science compelled me to devise superlative means to murder— what's that but sin against the Holy Christ? The unforgivable sin."[6] We have already seen that in *The New Men,* C. P. Snow uses the bombings of Hiroshima and Nagasaki as the catalyst for the scientist-hero's similar moral revulsion against his own work in atomic-weapons research.

Clearly, each of these novels transcends the specific issue of Hiroshima and Nagasaki to raise the larger question of the use of nuclear weapons in general. In each case, someone closely connected with the production of these weapons resigns his position because he feels they represent a new kind of threat to the existence of humanity—a threat that cannot be justified by any argument. This sense of the essential immorality of nuclear weapons provides the foundation for Aldous Huxley's 1947 novel *Ape and Essence.* The novel is written in the form of a film script, and the earliest images are a surrealistic rendering of the history of the atomic age. Huxley shows us two groups of apes who dress like human beings and lead around on chains men who resemble Albert Einstein. The two groups are warring factions who force the Einsteins to make weapons that will eliminate the other side. Of course, because each side has these weapons, both are destroyed. Clearly Huxley feels that man is, at heart, a brute being with savage impulses. Instead of using his science to improve his state, he allows the brute impulses to dominate and to pervert his knowledge toward destructive ends.

This concept is refined later in the novel when a survivor of the nuclear war, a priest of Satan, explains his philosophy of human history: "As I read history . . . it's like this. Man pitting himself against Nature, the Ego against the Order of Things, Belial . . . against the Other One. For a hundred thousand years or so the battle's entirely indecisive. Then, three centuries ago, almost overnight, the tide starts to run uninterruptedly in one direction. . . . Slowly at first, and then with gathering momentum, man begins to make headway against the Order of Things" (120).[7] He goes on to detail how man, in his pursuit of "progress" looked to industrialization, which ultimately led to dehumanization, overpopulation, hunger, disease, and death. He also points out that progress is the "midwife of force," and inevitably leads to war. Science, of course, also insured "progress" in war, developing bigger and better machines of death including, ultimately, the atomic bomb: "And finally, of course, there was the Thing. . . . And it all happened without any miracle or special intervention. . . . By purely natural means, using human beings and their science as His instruments, He created an entirely new race of men, with deformity in their blood, with squalor all around them and ahead, in the future, no prospects but of more squalor, worse deformity and, finally, complete extinction" (132–133).

Huxley's argument does more than attack nuclear weapons. It takes aim at nationalism, industrialism, and dehumanizing science as well. But in explicitly linking the atomic bomb to these issues and by using a representation of ultimate evil to symbolize the diabolical spirit that gives rise to them, Huxley does argue powerfully for the abolition of nuclear weapons. If they are the most recent and most dramatic manifestation of the worship of Belial, eliminating them might be a logical place to start an attempt to counteract mankind's suicidal tendencies.

This conviction of the basic immorality of all nuclear weapons is also central to the theme of Walter M. Miller, Jr.'s *A Canticle for*

Leibowitz. A significant part of the debate carried on in the book concerns the responsibility of science for the power it gives to man. Miller questions whether scientists can ignore their moral responsibility in giving nuclear capabilities to mankind when they know that mankind will almost certainly misuse those capabilities. This issue is debated by the abbot of a monastery which has preserved a remnant of twentieth-century knowledge after a nuclear war and a secular scientist who is attempting to usher in a new renaissance twelve centuries after that war. While the scientist coldly admits that some people, of necessity, will be destroyed in the effort to build the new world, the abbot is not so willing to concede the inevitability of this price: "But who will govern the use of the power to control natural forces? Who will use it? To what end? How will you hold him in check? Such decisions can still be made. But if you and your group don't make them now, others will soon make them for you" (206–7). Of course, the fact that this discussion is taking place twelve hundred years after nuclear war has all but destroyed civilization validates the abbot's argument. Since man has already used the power of science irresponsibly once, the scientist cannot ignore the probability that he will do so again. And the scientist's attempt to dismiss his moral responsibility for the knowledge he finds strikes the reader as criminal folly.

Moreover, as Hoban does in *Riddley Walker,* Miller links the misuse of power that nuclear war represents with basic flaws in the nature of man, this time in a specifically religious context. In an effort to influence the scientist's attitude toward the dissemination of scientific knowledge, one of the monks recites an account of the holocaust that destroyed civilization in the twentieth century. Because records of the war are fragmentary, however, the account takes the form of a biblical myth:

> And Satan spoke unto a certain prince, saying: "Fear not to use the sword for the wise men have deceived you in saying the world would be destroyed thereby. . . .
> And the prince did not heed the word of Satan, and . . . smote the cities of his enemies with the new fire. . . .
> And a great stink went up from the Earth even unto Heaven. . . . The stink of the carnage was exceedingly offensive to the Lord, Who spoke unto the prince *Name,* saying: "WHAT BURNT OFFERING IS THIS THAT YOU HAVE PREPARED BEFORE ME? . . .
> But the prince answered him not, and God said: "YOU HAVE MADE ME A HOLOCAUST OF MY SONS". (170–72)

This schematic rendering of the origins of a nuclear war, with its veneer of traditional biblical language, its specific reference to the faithfulness of Job—a faithfulness that modern man fails to imitate—and its echoes of the stories of Adam and Eve and Cain and Abel, all help to establish Miller's contention that the root cause of the problem of nuclear weapons is mans' fallen nature. The inherent capacity of man for sin—and for repentance—remains constant in the several centuries that the plot takes to play itself out. What changes is man's technological capacities—capacities that ultimately combine with his fallen nature to destroy the civilization that has been slowly and painfully rebuilt throughout the novel. Miller's point is that, given man's history, it is unreasonable to expect him to be able to control the overwhelming power of the atom. His nature is too flawed to do so. Thus, giving nuclear weapons to man is a hopelessly irresponsible act which ultimately dooms the human race to destruction.

Clearly, then, *A Canticle for Leibowitz* points up the essential immorality of nuclear weapons, implying that such weapons should not be deployed or even researched. At the same time, however, the novel provides the most elaborate fictional rendering of another great theme of the nuclear debate: the impossibility of ridding the world of nuclear weapons. From the beginning of the nuclear age in 1945, scientists pointed out that, even if the leaders of the Earth's nations were wise enough to abolish nuclear weapons, the knowledge of how to make them could never really be eliminated. Therefore, the weapons would remains taboo only while political accommodations existed between nations. If war broke out between two nations that possessed nuclear capabilities, nothing would stop those nations from rearming. Indeed, they would feel compelled to rearm for fear that the enemy was redeveloping nuclear weapons. Furthermore, even if all the books that contained the information necessary to build nuclear weapons could be destroyed and every person who knew anything about the process could be silenced, the potential for nuclear fission and fusion is a constant of physical law. The secret could always be rediscovered.

A Canticle for Leibowitz demonstrates how indestructible the knowledge of making nuclear weapons is. According to Miller's account, man destroys his civilization through nuclear war sometime in the latter part of the twentieth century. Enraged at what science has done, the common people attempt to destroy all knowledge of the weapons by burning books and killing the scientists who developed the knowledge. One nuclear scientist,

Isaac Leibowitz, is protected from the mobs by a group of monks. He eventually sets up his own religious order with the express purpose of salvaging man's knowledge from obscurity and preserving it through the new Dark Ages until man wants it again. The first part of the novel takes place six hundred years after these events when the monks find the remains of a fallout shelter in which a number of Leibowitz's colleagues died. Within the shelter they discover scientific documents, including a blueprint for part of a nuclear device. Given their mission in life, the monks preserve the information in their abbey, awaiting the time when someone will come to integrate it with other bits of knowledge.

Another six hundred years passes before that time comes. Thon Tadeo Pfardentrott visits the abbey to study the ancient documents in order to advance the cause of science. Even he is impressed by the amount of knowledge that the monks have been able to preserve: among the documents is a full explanation of Einstein's theory of relativity. Clearly, the information he finds, combined with his own considerable talents as a research scientist, will give the burgeoning second renaissance a great thrust forward. The problem, as we have already seen, is that Thon Taddeo makes no effort to insure that the knowledge he is reintroducing to the world will be used responsibly. He himself scorns the religious values that lead the abbot of the monastery to warn him of the dangers of putting enormous power in the hands of flawed mankind, and he is financed and controlled by his cousin, the despotic, power-hungry King Hannegan II. The stage is set for another cycle of scientific growth climaxed by another calamity.

That calamity comes in the third section of the novel which takes place in 3781. Civilization has now risen up to and beyond the technological level of the twentieth century. Unfortunately, this level of technology includes the existence of more powerful nuclear weapons. Once again, man destroys his planet with these weapons, but this time the only hope for his continued existence lies in fleeing to colonies on other planets. In order to continue the effort to help man battle his fallen nature, the Order of St. Leibowitz sends a self-sustaining community to these colonies. Miller is suggesting that, given the persistence of the knowledge of nuclear weapons, mankind's history will consist of ongoing cycles of destruction, slow rebirth, and renewed destruction unless man learns to control the negative aspects of his nature. If the laws of physics must remain the same, then man's response to his basic nature must change.

Not everyone who has confronted the inevitability of nuclear technology, however, has suggested large-scale changes in man's nature in order to control the threat of nuclear weapons. Indeed, more people have looked toward systemic solutions to the nuclear crisis. One of the earliest proposed resolutions of the problem was a ban on war in general. If there were no wars, then there would be no use for the atomic bomb. In fact, many believed that the terrors of nuclear destruction would serve to end war. General Henry H. Arnold, commander of the Army Air Forces, publicly made this suggestion as early as August 1945: "This thing is so terrible in its aspects that there may not be any more wars."[8] George Bernard Shaw echoed this hopeful view in the first two sections of his *Farfetched Fables* in the late 1940s.

Those who advocated the abolition of war, however, were taking on a problem even more formidable than banning the bomb. War has been a staple of man's behavior throughout history. Even those who cite the fact that the nations of the world have refrained from total war over the past forty years must admit that the threat of nuclear catastrophe has not entirely quashed man's aggressiveness. Indeed, the number of localized conflicts since 1945—in Korea, in Vietnam, in Central and South America, in Afghanistan, in Cambodia, and so on—suggest that mankind either is hopelessly addicted to warfare or is desperately in need of a humane vehicle for solving international conflicts.

One such vehicle—world government—has long been a dream of many people. The first actual movement toward it, in fact, predated the use of nuclear weapons by thirty years when the League of Nations was formed after World War I. In principle, this body was to arbitrate international disputes and guarantee international order. In actuality the League had little power and even lacked the cooperation of the United States, whose president, Woodrow Wilson, had urged the concept on the victorious Allies in 1917. The failure of the League was most obvious, of course, in its inability to prevent World War II. That war, however, gave rise to the second and, to some extent, more successful attempt at world government in this century—the United Nations. Once again, the UN was an attempt to settle international disputes without resort to war and to establish a unified code of international behavior. Those who founded it saw it as the beginning of the end of all war, and the advent of the nuclear age underlined the importance of achieving such a goal. As we have seen, however, the UN did not sound permanent retreat for the armies of the world. Nevertheless, those who have felt the need to deal with the nuclear threat in some final, effective way have continued to look to world government as the solution to man's greatest problem. It is the solution that Bertrand Russell outlines in *Has Man a Future?* He calls for the absolute abolition of independent nations to the point that children would be taught loyalty, not to their native countries, but to the world community. This goal is also at the heart of Jonathan Schell's 1982 book, *The Fate of the Earth.*

Naturally the concept of world government as a solution to the nuclear threat found its way into fiction. As we have seen, Huxley attacked the whole concept of nationalism in *Ape and Essence* as early as 1947. In 1951 the theme was presented to a wider audience in a popular science fiction film *The Day the Earth Stood Still.* The film gives us a man from outer space who warns the human race of the cosmic dangers posed by the combination of nuclear weapons and rocket technology. He cites the example of the more advanced planets, which he represents, in suggesting how the nations of the Earth might solve their problems:

> The universe grows smaller every day, and the threat of aggression by any group anywhere can no longer be tolerated. . . . We have an organization for the mutual protection of all planets and for the complete elimination of aggression. . . . For our policemen we created a race of robots. . . . The result is we live in peace, without arms or armies, secure in the knowledge that we are free from aggression and war. . . . Your choice is simple: join us and live in peace, or pursue your present course and face obliteration. . . . The decision rests with you.[9]

If we replace the fantastic universal federation of planets with a hypothetically possible world federation of nations, we see that the director, Robert Wise, is symbolically proposing a more powerful version of the UN, whose principal function is to keep peace between nations, although not necessarily within them. The suggestion that the Earth could be reduced to cinders if the federation is not adopted foresees a time when the nations of the Earth would have sufficient nuclear weapons to destroy the planet. The notion of the race of robots built to enforce order in the universe, of course, implies that the UN must have some form of effective coercive power to enforce order in the world. While, in reality, the UN has been unable to establish such a coercive power, the statement that the robots' action is too terrible to risk might be a reference to a plan to turn control of all nuclear weapons over to the organization. If this action were taken, not only could individual nations not use the weapons against each other, the UN could use them to force recalcitrant nations to accept arbitration of international disputes. Such a plan had actually been put before the UN by the United States in 1946, but had been rejected by the Soviet Union.[10] When the Soviets developed the atomic bomb themselves, all hope of international control was abandoned on both sides, and the arms race was engaged.

It is interesting that *The Day the Earth Stood Still* could argue for a position that had become very controversial by 1951. The stand it takes is especially surprising when one remembers that it was made during the height of the Communist witch hunts, which had an enormous impact on Hollywood. Of course, the method Wise used to avoid political problems was to employ fantasy to distance the immediate impact of what he was saying from the real world. Instead of having a world leader get up and propose an international government, he manufactured a fantastic analog for such an action. By doing so he allowed the audience to analyze the proposal in the abstract and come to some conclusion about its desirability without feeling constrained by current political propaganda. If their conclusions were favorable, they would be more disposed to accept an actual proposal for effective world government when it came, without dismissing it as some form of Communist plot. Thus, *The Day the Earth Stood Still* exemplifies the ability of fiction to mask its true persuasive intent when necessary and argue its case symbolically in order to avoid ingrained but baseless objections to what it is proposing.

By the time Ben Bova wrote *Millennium* in 1976, it was no longer necessary to mask an appeal for world government. Even though he uses fantastic elements in telling his story, Bova explicitly argues for world government as the only hope for the survival of mankind. The plot concerns the efforts of the commander of an American moon base to avoid being drawn into an American-Soviet nuclear conflict. Together with the commander of the adjacent Soviet base, he establishes an independent nation on the moon, which he intends to defend by taking over the American and Soviet antimissile satellites. When he discovers that these satellites can also be used to control the weather on Earth, he decides that they could be used to give the UN the power to maintain international order. While, of course, the regulatory force with which Bova empowers the UN does not exist, he succeeds in making his point: only through international action—through some form of world government—can the threat of nuclear annihilation be laid to rest.

Unfortunately, the nations of the world did not decide to institute international control of their nuclear weapons. Instead they allowed mutual suspicion and fear to condition their reactions. As soon as Stalin learned that the United States had developed the atomic bomb, he ordered his scientists to increase their efforts to develop such a weapon.[11] Immediately after the bombings of Japan, when the United States had a monopoly on atomic weapons and had nothing to fear from any other nation on Earth, the army recommended the development of an arsenal of over four hundred nuclear weapons.[12] The implication of this recommendation was that the United States should consider nuclear weapons as valid instruments for the conduct of foreign policy. And, indeed, on some occasions the weapons were used as just that. The most notable instance occurred shortly after Dwight Eisenhower became president in 1953. He subtly threatened the use of atomic weapons in Korea if the war continued to drag on. Even though the Soviets had developed the bomb by that time, the United States still had an overwhelming nuclear superiority, and by July of 1953 a truce was signed. Secretary of State John Foster Dulles later credited the threat with ending the Korean War.[13]

The fear of just such threats had been at least partially behind the Soviets' own rush to develop the bomb in the late 1940s, and the materialization of the threats no doubt spurred them to try to keep up with the Americans in the arms race. However, their development of the atom bomb in 1949 caused the United States to decide to build a hydrogen bomb, which they successfully tested in 1952.[14] Terrified of falling behind once again, the Soviets developed their own hydrogen bomb by 1954.[15] At the same time the two nations were also rushing to stay ahead of each other in developing quicker and more accurate delivery systems for the weapons—improved bombers and, later, missiles. Of course, none of these developments, of themselves, could keep either side safe from the other's nuclear weapons. Instead, the weapons were developed and deployed to provide a counterthreat to the other's threat. If one side used nuclear weapons, the other side would use its own to destroy the aggressor. The theory behind this dynamic was formalized in the early 1960s by Secretary of State Robert McNamara who gave it a name in 1967: Mutual Assured Destruction or MAD. Each side knew that if it used its weapons it would be committing an act of national suicide. The United States and the Soviet Union were locked into what McNamara referred to as a "balance of terror."[16]

Despite its cold-blooded logic, the strategy of Mutual Assured

Destruction had much to recommend it, at least on a theoretical level. Many policymakers argued that the threat of ultimate annihilation was necessary to curb the aggressive tendencies of the Soviet Union. Given this premise, they felt that it was equally necessary for the United States to announce its resolve to carry out that destruction if necessary. Even those who were uncomfortable with the concept for humanitarian or moral reasons had to admit that it did provide at least some immediate solution to the problems of the potential use of nuclear weapons. As long as both sides realized that using the weapons was an act of suicide, no sane leader would do so. The policy made nuclear war too terrible and too final for anyone to want to risk it. On a more mundane but immediately practical level, it actually reduced the need for nuclear weapons. Once a government had enough weapons to destroy a certain percentage of the enemy's cities, population, and production facilities, it would not need to add to the arsenal.

But from the start, the policy had its opponents as well as its supporters. Some found the concept unacceptable because they felt it was, at base, immoral and unethical for two great countries to maintain the peace by constantly threatening to destroy the civilian populations of its enemies. Others had less altruistic reasons for opposing MAD. Some saw it as a strategy that robbed a nation of a viable defense option—limited nuclear war. Herman Kahn, for example, suggested a whole range of responses to enemy aggression, from negotiation, through the use of conventional weapons and the limited use of nuclear weapons, and finally to full-scale nuclear war. He also warned that even a relatively stable balance of terror does not completely eliminate the potential for war.[17] Kahn proposed the analogy of the Doomsday Device in order to point up the danger of MAD: "Assume that for say, ten billion dollars we could build a device whose only function is to destroy all human life. The device is . . . connected to a computer which is in turn connected, by a reliable communications system, to hundreds of sensory devices all over the United States. The computer would then be programmed so that if, say, five nuclear bombs exploded over the United States, the device would be triggered and the Earth destroyed."[18] He goes on to point out that the device would fulfill most of the requirements for a credible deterrent: it would be frightening, inexorable, persuasive, cheap, and nonaccident prone. It would not have another necessary quality of a stable deterrent, however: it would not be controllable. It could not be disarmed in the event of an actual strike. Therefore, it something happened by accident, it could lead to the destruction of the world. Kahn felt that MAD, taken to its logical conclusion, was the equivalent of such a device.

It might be asked, of course, how MAD could possibly fail given a situation of stable deterrence. The most common answer has been accidental war caused by either technological or human failure. In *Missile Envy* Caldicott speaks of 152 incidents from January 1979 to June 1980 in which the United States' early warning system indicated that Soviet missiles might be attacking. Of these, 149 were the result of the failure of infrared sensors on U.S. satellites to discriminate properly between actual launches and harmless phenomena. Two others were caused by computer malfunction, and the last by a technician's mistakenly loading a war games tape into a computer.[19] Both she and Dyson cite the historical volatility of the human character as a threat of accidental war, noting the number of madmen who have become heads of state. A madman at the head of a nuclear state, they point out, could easily bring about Armageddon.

All of these objections to MAD have found their way into the fiction of nuclear war. The moral and psychological debilitation of living with the kill-and-be-killed attitude of MAD provides the theme of *Level 7*, for example. The novel presents a world in which the two major nuclear powers are equally well-armed. Logically, neither side can make a move against the other without committing suicide. The strategy of Mutual Assured Destruction would consider them to be in a state of perfect stable deterrence and would judge this situation to be ideal. What is clearly not ideal is the life of those who inhabit Level 7. As we have seen, the people on Level 7 are trapped there—condemned to live in this subterranean world for the rest of their lives. Also they have been sent to Level 7 without their consent, realizing their plight only after their arrival. Their lives are controlled by faceless voices who are not elected, but who claim to have the security of the state at heart. Most of all, while the rules of Level 7 have their own consistent internal logic, they are ultimately dehumanizing.

In many ways, life on Level 7 is symbolic of life in a country armed with nuclear weapons. Like the inhabitants of Level 7, we find ourselves trapped in a condition that daily threatens us and reduces the joy of life. At the same time, we see our survival as dependent on threatening our enemies and forcing them to live in the same kind of trap. Like Level 7 the nuclear strategic balance has become the environment in which we live our lives. We follow the principles of deterrence—the strategy of Mutual Assured Destruction—and those principles have their own consistent internal logic. But that logic, upon close examination, reveals itself to be inhuman and even insane. We hold elections, leaders change, but the principles that govern life in the nuclear age remain the same. Parity, stability, deterrence, assured destruction—all are part of the common vocabulary of Democrat and Republican, liberal and conservative.

If we accept the idea that Level 7 is a symbol of our own world, we may begin to see how the debilitating effects of Level 7 on its inhabitants parallel the impact of MAD on us. The sense of limits that life on Level 7 necessarily imposes, depresses even the most ardent believers in the system. As X-127 notes, man needs a sense of the infinite—a sense that life can stretch beyond the visible horizon. Stripped of this quality of life, man begins to lose his sense of humanity. Of course, the rulers of Level 7 have attempted to meet this danger of dehumanization. They provide psychiatrists to work their magic of modern medicine on the inhabitants. But the psychiatrists themselves are compromised by their own growing angst. Level 7 also attempts to provide a sense of normalcy by continuing key social relationships, most importantly by urging its inhabitants to marry, even instituting an appropriately sterile ceremony to celebrate the marriages. Theoretically, the aims of Level 7 and the demands of the human personality should come together in these unions. Level 7 wants to maintain stabilizing social relationships and provide itself a second generation of inhabitants. The stable relationships could remind the inhabitants what it is to be a human being, and the second generation could give them the sense of the infinite that they need. But the depressing basic assumptions of Level 7 itself counteract any possible advantages of these relationships, and most of the marriages break up. X-127 himself marries a psychological officer, but he finds no comfort in the relationship.

At the same time that their own lives have become circumscribed and cheapened by Level 7, some of the inhabitants worry about the moral implications of their condition. As we have seen in a previous chapter, X-127 has nightmares about his mother's being killed in nuclear explosions. He also worries if his supposed psychological fitness for Level 7 indicates a fundamental flaw in his own personality: "Why can I not care more for other people?—people up there or people down here, it does not matter which. It is as if my soul were deformed or part of it had been amputated" (47). This moral uneasiness is shared by many members of the community. X-117, to cite the most extreme case, suffers severe psychological problems as a result of his alienation from his loved ones. He eventually breaks down completely and commits suicide out of guilt for his part in the destruction of the world. Before he does so, he reproaches the psychological officer: "So you've had enough of this visit, you psychologist, you soul killer! You managed to cure me of my conscience so that I'd be able to kill humanity" (110).

All of these psychological and moral problems are humanity's legacy in the nuclear age. If we need a sense of the limitless to be fully human, clearly the constant possibility of imminent destruction that MAD mandates must do something to our humanity. And if one of the most basic laws in the canon of Western society is "Thou shalt not kill," the fact that we have chosen to defend ourselves by threatening the wholesale slaughter of innocent civilians must be a moral evil that, ultimately, we cannot ignore.

Other works attack the efficacy of the strategy of Mutual Assured Destruction by attempting to show how it could break down and what would happen if it did. *Fail-Safe*, for example, deals with a technological failure that almost leads to accidental war. The event begins when the Strategic Air Command's radar detects an unidentified object encroaching on American air space. According to routine, U.S. bombers are ordered to their fail-safe points—fixed areas in the sky near Russian air space—to await further orders. Just when the American commanders discover that the object is an off-course airliner, however, a malfunction in the computer that controls the fail-safe system orders one bomber wing to attack Moscow. Detecting this movement, the Soviet commanders, responding to suggestions from their computers, block radio contact between the wing and its base, frustrating any attempt to inject a human control into the situation. Thus, the incident is precipitated by a machine's malfunction, which itself vitiates the basic assumptions of the safety of MAD, and is perpetuated on the Soviet side by human response to another machine.

All through these various events, the inability of the human being to gain control of his machines is emphasized. At one point in the novel, a congressman, a systems manufacturer, and two military men attempt to settle the question of human accountability. When the congressman asks who has ultimate responsibility for the system, the soldiers say the president does, but the manufacturer contends that, in reality, no one does. Essentially, this statement is true. William M. Arkin and Richard W. Fieldhouse of the Institute for Policy Studies note that, given the complexity of nuclear warfare and the short time in which decisions must be made, "the ability of humans to manage the whole nuclear apparatus at a central location diminishes."[20] Thus, the president will have less and less control over the decision-making process, and the machines themselves will grow more and more important. The problem with this state of affairs is that the machines may malfunction. The manufacturer in Burdick and Wheeler's *Fail-Safe* admits this possibility: "The more complex an electronics system gets, the more accident prone it is. . . . Take our missiles. . . . The Atlas is the most reliable missile we possess. But what happens: we make our first moon shot and it misses by 25,000 miles" (186–87).

This argument, backed up as it is with specific references to actual weapons systems, asserts that an accidental strike is not only possible, but inevitable. Of course, the action of the novel verifies the validity of this argument. The logic of MAD, however, does not allow for accidental nuclear strikes. The strategy would insist that, in the case put in the novel, the Soviets should launch a full strike against the United States as soon as the bombs destroyed Moscow. It would also demand that the United States, observing this attack, launch one of its own, laying waste to the Soviet Union. In the end, the two greatest powers on Earth would have destroyed each other because of a faulty component in a weapons system.

In point of fact, however, this scenario does not occur in the novel. The president of the United States manages to convince the Soviet premier that the destruction of Moscow was an accident, but only by ordering one of his own generals to drop two hydrogen bombs on New York City. As horrifying as this solution is, some might argue that it weakens the point of the book by allowing the United States and the Soviet Union to survive the accidental strike. The reader might be left with the inference that MAD is not the great danger that its opponents claim it is, since the example presented allows human understanding to override the cold logic of the strategy. Such an objection, however, ignores the basic dramatic terms of Burdick and Wheeler's argument. As an object lesson, *Fail-Safe* does present us with a picture of mutual destruction. Granted, the destruction is not on the vast level that MAD calls for—it does not destroy the two countries as functioning twentieth-century nations. But it does destroy the two greatest cities of those nations—the two cities that more than any others symbolize them. The crucial point is that the sacrifice of New York at the end of the novel will not restore Moscow, just as full-scale retaliation against an aggressor would not restore the attacked country in a nuclear war. The dynamic may be presented in microcosm, but the point that it is senseless and brutal has been made. Moreover, because the president has had to order the destruction of his own city, we see the essential suicidal nature of MAD. Just as the dropping of the hydrogen bombs on Moscow also condemns New York, any attack on a nuclear rival—whether by design or by accident—insures the destruction of the attacker.

Stanley Kubrick's *Dr. Strangelove* attacks the logic of MAD by concentrating on the other great threat of accidental nuclear war— an unauthorized strike generated by human failure. As a result of fears about a Communist plot to subvert the United States by contaminating the bodily fluids of its citizens, an insane Air Force base commander named General Jack D. Ripper sends his wing to bomb the Soviet Union. Knowing that the strategy of MAD would cause the Soviets to respond to such an attack with full retaliation and knowing that the president and the Pentagon realize this fact, Ripper hopes they will feel compelled to join the full might of American military power to his renegade attack in order to annihi- late the Soviets' retaliatory capacity before being annihilated themselves. Thus, the weaknesses of MAD are central to the action of *Dr. Strangelove*.

Despite the satirical intent that pushes characters and events up to and past the level of caricature, there is an underlying plau- sibility to the film that points up specific dangers of the doctrine of MAD. It is true, for example, that people other than the president may possess the actual power to use nuclear weapons. In the event of the president's death, the authority to order nuclear retaliation automatically passes to the next person in the chain of command—the Vice-president, then the speaker of the House of Representatives, and so on. Edward Zuckerman points out that, because communication with submarines is difficult in times of crisis, submarine commanders are able to launch nuclear weap- ons without submitting to the same sorts of checks and balances that those who control ground-based missiles must. It is conceiv- able—although, according to Zuckerman, unlikely—that a de- ranged submarine commander could launch the sort of strike portrayed in *Dr. Strangelove*.[21] In addition, the United States has deployed over three thousand tactical nuclear weapons of various sizes throughout Europe intended to be used if conventional resistance to Soviet aggression is insufficient.[22] Of course, there are strict controls over the use of these weapons, but those con- trols are, of necessity, not as strict as those on strategic weapons. Once again, such weapons are in the hands of line commanders who could presumably use them even without proper authorization.

In order to accept the plausibility of Kubrick's scenario, however, the audience must be convinced not only that powers under the president could have the physical ability to launch some kind of nuclear strike, but also that they could have lost their senses sufficiently to do so. There is some evidence to indicate that this case is also possible. The United States government, recognizing the dangers of an unreliable person's being involved with nuclear weapons, does have a program that attempts to screen out unstable people and prevent them from working with nuclear weapons in any capacity. Helen Caldicott points out that from 1975 to 1977 people were removed from the reliability lists at the rate of 4 percent per year. In 1977 about three-quarters of those removals were for abuse of drugs such as alcohol, marijuana, heroin, and LSD. About one-quarter were removed for "significant mental, physical, or character trait or aberrant behavior substantiated by competent medical authorities," which might "prejudice reliable performance of the particular duties of a particular controlled condition."[23] While some might cite these removals as evidence that the system works, critics might point out that the individuals removed *were* authorized to work with nuclear weapons until their instability was discovered. They might also ask whether any psychological screening system can be as absolutely foolproof as one involving the possible destruction of Western civilization must be. Kubrick plays on this point when, in a discussion of such a screening system, he has General Turgidsen say, "Well, I don't think it's fair to condemn a whole program because of a single slip-up." The biting satire of the line is based on the irony that in an imperfect world MAD places the only hope for survival on absolute perfection.

Despite the apparent absurdity of some of the characters, then, Kubrick's film *is* designed as a plausible satire of a specific danger of MAD—the possibility that war could be triggered by the monumental miscalculation of someone who is unwilling or unable to see its suicidal nature. But in making real Herman Kahn's metaphor of the "doomsday device," Kubrick expands his attack from the specific to the general. Ultimately, the audience sees that his target is the basic thinking behind the strategy.

Halfway through the film, the Soviet premier informs President Merkin Muffley that if even one American plane of Ripper's wing is able to penetrate Soviet defenses and drop its bombs, it will trigger a doomsday device: fifty-one hundred megaton hydrogen bombs jacketed with "debalthorium three," an element with a radioactive half-life of ninety-three years. As the Soviet ambassador warns, when the bombs go off they will contaminate the earth's atmosphere with lethal fallout for nearly a century. When the president asks if it is possible to trigger such a device automatically, his science advisor Dr. Strangelove, delivers an answer that parallels Kahn's own account of a doomsday device:

> [B]ecause of the automated and irrevocable decision-making process which rules out human meddling, the Doomsday Machine is terrifying and simple to understand and completely convincing. . . . When you only wish to bury bombs, there's no limit to the size. After that they are connected to a gigantic complex of computers. Now then, a specific and clearly defined set of circumstances under which the bombs are to be exploded are programmed into the taped memory bank.

Of course, Strangelove's familiarity with the concept comes from firsthand experience; as weapons consultant he had ordered a study by the "Bland Corporation" into the feasibility of such a system. Ultimately he rejected the concept "for reasons that at this moment should be all too obvious." The obvious reason is, as Kahn would say, that the doomsday machine lacks an important component of a credible deterrent: it is not controllable.

Clearly, then, *Dr. Strangelove* is an attack on the basic strategic concepts of its—and our—day by suggesting what civilization's future would be if somehow the "balance of terror" were accidentally breached. And to emphasize the horror of man's plight, Kubrick does not even supply the modicum of hope that the authors of *Fail-Safe* do. Instead of adopting some scenario that would allow him to make his point without destroying the world, Kubrick plays out the logic of the doomsday device—and the MAD strategy. The final images of the film are a montage of nuclear explosions which, presumably, will blanket the world with deadly levels of debalthorium three for the following ninety-three years.

Despite arguments such as these, Mutual Assured Destruction has remained the official strategy of the United States for at least twenty years. On a practical level, however, decisions about weapons systems during that period have been based increasingly on a strategy of enabling the United States to fight a limited nuclear war. As we have seen, Kahn opposed MAD principally because the strategy eliminated a whole range of alternatives to Soviet aggressions, including limited use of nuclear weapons. He insisted that they be placed in the arsenal of democracy along with conventional weapons, the difference being considered one of degree rather than kind. Thus, he justified the deployment of an array of nuclear weapons ranging from the tactical to the strategic and recommended intricate but flexible strategies that would govern their actual use. This concept has been labeled the strategy of Limited Nuclear War or Nuclear War Fighting.

Official policy statements aside, the concept of limited nuclear was has long been a part of the United States' strategic thinking. When we had a monopoly on nuclear weapons in the late 1940s, policymakers had no difficulty in seeing them as viable instruments of enforcing our national will on the world. We have already seen how threats of nuclear intervention helped Eisenhower bring the Korean War to an end. Barry Goldwater created a controversy during the 1964 presidential election by urging that NATO commanders be authorized to use tactical nuclear weapons during crises.[24] Richard Nixon apparently threatened their use in Vietnam in the late 1960s and early 1970s.[25] Moreover, such uses would not really have represented aberrations from ongoing policy. While the United States does maintain a policy of Mutual Assured Destruction in relation to strategic nuclear weapons, its plans for the defense of Western Europe are heavily predicated on the possibility of the limited use of tactical nuclear weapons—types with yields so low that their effects would theoretically be limited to the battlefield.

The concept that actual limited exchanges of strategic nuclear weapons are possible without insuring the destruction of the two countries involved has infiltrated policymakers' thinking gradually over the past twenty years. The theory of strategic nuclear war fighting states that, given proper command and control systems and viable diplomatic channels, the two sides in a nuclear exchange could employ their weapons judiciously and be able to disengage the conflict before fatal damage was done to the infrastructure of civilization. The justification of this theory lies in the sort of targeting the strategy mandates. MAD depends on "countervalue" targeting which means that the enemies aim at each other's cities and industries. Nuclear War Fighting presumes a different kind of targeting called "counterforce" targeting. In this strategy, the participants aim at the enemy's weapons—primarily their nuclear weapons—hoping to destroy them completely before they can be launched.[26]

The advantages of a Nuclear War Fighting capacity based on counterforce targeting seem obvious. Instead of holding the enemy's civilians hostage, so to speak, a country aims to destroy the most dangerous of its enemy's weapons with a minimum loss of civilian life. On the surface, at least, this strategy seems at once more humane in its approach to the enemy and potentially more effective in protecting a country's own population. It is more clearly a defensive strategy than MAD in that it concentrates on destroying the enemy's real threat before it is used than on exacting unacceptable revenge on the enemy's people after the enemy has already destroyed one's own country. It would seem to provide a more acceptable response to the threat of nuclear war than does Mutual Assured Destruction.

In line with the convoluted logic that is ingrained in the nuclear debate, however, those who most oppose nuclear weapons prefer the concept of Mutual Assured Destruction to a strategy of Limited Nuclear War. The reason for this attitude is simple: in making nuclear war less total, Nuclear War Fighting strategies make it less terrifying and, therefore, more likely. Despite the dangers of accidental war, MAD at least has the virtue of declaring any use of nuclear weapons unacceptable for a sane, responsible nation, if only because such a use would seal the user's own fate. Nuclear War Fighting, however, again opens the door for the use of these weapons as legitimate instruments of national policy.

Opponents maintain that any use of nuclear weapons, even the limited use that Nuclear War Fighting envisions, would be disastrous beyond measure for the people in the vicinity of the targets. An even greater problem would be the level of fallout that counterforce targeting would create. In order to destroy hardened missile silos, nuclear weapons would have to be detonated at ground level. These ground bursts would create much more radioactive fallout than air bursts, thereby increasing the long-range and long-term effects of the attack. Another objection is that the term "Limited Nuclear War" sounds much more civilized than "Mutual Assured Destruction." For this reason, opponents fear that leaders would be psychologically much more able to launch a limited strike than a full-scale attack. Of course, there is no guarantee that a limited strike would stay limited. Once the absolute prohibition against using the weapons was breached, opponents of nuclear weapons fear that use would grow uncontrollably until mutual destruction was realized.

Indeed, all sides of the nuclear debate seem to agree that the most likely scenario for the onslaught of nuclear war would not include a "bolt out of the blue" strike by one side on the other. Instead it would much more likely be the result of a protracted

international crisis in some sensitive spot like Western Europe or
the Middle East. The sequence of events would begin with some
diplomatic dispute involving territorial claims and threatened
troop movements. Some conventional action might be taken—for
example, a Soviet invasion of West Germany. Faced with the
Soviets' overwhelming conventional superiority in the area,
NATO forces might be faced with the option of succumbing to a
latter-day *blitzkrieg* or of using various kinds of tactical nuclear
weapons to stem the invasion. Presuming that NATO commanders felt they could use such weapons without fear that the
conflict would escalate into full-scale nuclear war, they would
probably pick the nuclear option. However, the Soviet Union's
policy is that they will answer any use of nuclear weapons against
them with an all-out response, including the use of their strategic
missiles.[27]

This scenario is almost precisely the one presented in *The Day
After*. While the film seems to compress into a few days a sequence of events that would, in reality, occur over the course of
weeks, director Nicholas Meyer seems determined to show as
realistically as possible how an actual nuclear conflict could arise
and escalate. To this end, the first reports of conflict in Europe are
introduced as largely ignored background activity to the everyday
lives of the people of Lawrence Kansas. Only as the dispute
escalates and leaders begin to hurl threats of war, do the characters become at first interested in and then frightened by the news.
Soviet troops approach a neutral border, and NATO troops go on
maneuvers. In Lawrence, the local missile base goes on alert and
an Air Force missile technician is forced to cancel vacation plans.
In Germany, an incursion of some sort is made, and NATO troops
fight back. East Germany launches a full-scale invasion of West
Germany, and students at the University of Kansas debate the
possibility of the United States' risking nuclear war to defend
Western Europe. The pace quickens and the news reports become
more emotional as a tactical nuclear weapon is detonated over
Eastern Bloc troops and another destroys a ship in the Persian
Gulf. Finally, intercontinental ballistic missiles rise out of their
Kansas silos, headed for the Soviet Union.

The point of the film is that the premises of limited nuclear war
are faulty. The first use of tactical nuclear weapons in Europe leads
inexorably to the obliteration of normal life in Lawrence, Kansas.
And, since we are told that over three hundred missiles have been
detected heading for the United States, we can assume that the
destruction has, in fact, been total. The number of missiles we

have seen on their way to the Soviet Union suggests further that the destruction is mutual.

The proponents of Nuclear War Fighting, of course, question the theory that any nuclear exchange would lead to full-scale strikes as well as the assertion that even large-scale nuclear strikes would lead to the complete destruction of the country. Even Jonathan Schell, whose *Fate of the Earth* suggests that life on Earth could be destroyed if even a moderate exchange between the United States and the Soviet Union occurred, admits that no one—not the scientists, not the military, not the politicians—really knows what would happen in such an exchange. In answer to this admittedly valid point, some opponents of Nuclear War Fighting have suggested that even the most limited nuclear war would bring about an unacceptable change in American life. According to this view, modern industrial society is so complex and delicate that even the smallest nuclear war would plunge the country into the middle ages. Edward Zuckerman's *The Day after World War III* details the government's plans to preserve the structure of society through a nuclear war and reveals how unrealistic those plans often are. For example, he quotes a memorandum by Gary Robbins, a Treasury Department planner, responding to a scenario that assumed nuclear weapons fell on only 25 percent of the country, including New York, Washington, Georgia, and the Western missile fields. Economically speaking, the actual blasts wiped out both the nation's facilities for producing money and its currency reserves, and the electromagnetic pulse destroyed computers vital to the tax system.[28] Added to this almost certain destruction of the economic underpinnings of society would be other problems: the contamination of the food chain, the probable decimation of local governments, and increased instances of disease arising from the reduction of health-care services. The effect of these various factors would be to end civilization as we know it in this country.

James Kunetka and Whitley Strieber's 1983 novel *Warday* is an effort to show the long-term effects of a nuclear exchange that is, if anything, more limited than that proposed in Robbins' memorandum. The authors postulate a nuclear exchange in 1988 initiated by the Soviets in response to the United States' efforts to deploy a defensive satellite system. Using weapons dropped from their own satellites, the Soviets first generate an electromagnetic pulse (EMP) which destroys the solid state circuits in computers and electronic equipment all across the country. Then they attempt to attack the principal cities and weapons bases. American retaliation is so swift and so similar, however, that the command and control systems on both sides are quickly destroyed, effectively eliminating within a few hours each side's capacity to carry on the war. In the United States—and presumably in the Soviet Union as well—only a fraction of the damage that MAD theory would postulate has actually occurred. We learn that New York City has been rendered uninhabitable by radiation, that Washington, D.C. and San Antonio, Texas have been annihilated, and that various missile fields in the Midwest have been destroyed. Other than these areas, however, most of the country has not been touched by direct blast effects. Given this relatively low level of apparent damage, the reader might at first conclude that the country could survive a limited war quite handily. Certainly he would have no trouble believing a 1972 Joint Chiefs of Staff study that predicted the country could recover from a nuclear war almost completely in six years.[29]

In the light of such predictions, it is significant that Strieber and Kunetka set the main part of their novel in 1992, five years after the war. As characters in their own fiction, the two authors set out on a journey to discover how well their ravaged country is actually recovering. What they find is not particularly encouraging to the proponents of Limited Nuclear War. Although relatively little of the country has been incinerated by the immediate effects of the weapons, it has all been affected to a much greater degree than most people might suspect.

As Zuckerman suggests in his book, the economy has been devastated. Strieber and Kunetka invent an economist who explains the consequences of a nuclear war on a complex economy: "All the money that was somehow in process in the computer systems of the government and private banks ceased to exist because of the electromagnetic disruption or, in the case of Washington, permanent and total destruction. That was about one dollar in ten, but it was all hypercritical money, because it was in motion. It was the liquid cash, what people were using to pay other people" (180).

One of the advantages of Strieber and Kunetka's method is that they combine their overviews and statistics with the stories of fictional people who exemplify them. In the case of the economy, they use their own imagined selves as exemplars. Before the war, they were both successful authors; now they are reduced to poverty. In their journey they have to smuggle themselves into California—a golden land almost untouched by the effects of the war—because they have so few financial assets. The incident is reminiscent of scenes in Steinbeck's *Grapes of Wrath*, and, indeed, Strieber and Kunetka seem to play repeatedly on images of the Great Depression. Apparently, they hope to suggest some sense of the horror of limited nuclear war by evoking memories, either direct or indirect, of the archetypal time of social suffering in our century.

Paralleling the breakdown of the economy is the collapse of central authority. Although the government of the United States nominally exists, it has relatively little power. For the most part, the elected government was incinerated at its desk, so to speak. Without a strong central authority to hold it together, the country has disintegrated into regions controlled by various power groups. California is a land unto itself, severely limiting immigration from the ravaged Midwest. Parts of Texas and Mexico have evolved into the Spanish-speaking country of Aztlan, which no longer recognizes the United States government. The South, like California, maintains a relatively robust economy and also treats attempts at immigration with hostility.

This fragmentation of the nation has retarded recovery from the war. Detroit does not produce even a fraction of the automobiles it did before the war, even though its factories were untouched by the devastation. Economic depression and lack of organization have combined to kill the industry. Agriculture is hampered by constant problems with radiation contamination and reduced productivity. The central government, of course, is powerless to help change these conditions. Instead foreign nations like Japan and Great Britain hold the key to the United States' recovery. These countries have fallen heir to the position of economic and industrial leadership of the Free World, and Americans are at their mercy in redeveloping their industrial capacity.

Still other long-range problems become issues in the novel. One is the ongoing effect of the war on the general health of the country. Various radiation-related illnesses—cancers, genetic mutations, unspecified new syndromes—are a major concern. At the same time the reduction in general hygiene and nutrition in areas affected by the war have left the population vulnerable to various illnesses ranging from cholera to flu. The most notable example of virulent disease mentioned is the Cincinnati Flu of 1990 which killed twenty-one million Americans. The incidence of illness, especially radiation-related illness, has so overwhelmed the capacities of the existing medical facilities that a system of triage has been instituted. Under this system, people whose "life dose" of radiation exceeds a certain level are permanently denied medical care under the presumption that they will almost certainly develop life-shortening illnesses so that medical help will ultimately be wasted on them. To bring this point home, the authors give Strieber an excess does of radiation during the war and often refer to the fact that he is legally prohibited from seeking medical care.

Above all, the country suffers the lingering aftereffects of a savage psychological blow. Paranoia is a recurring feature of the authors' conversations with the people they meet in their travels. A large percentage of the populace is convinced that someone somewhere is out to get them. Some fear that the Soviets have survived the war relatively unscathed and are about to launch an invasion. Others are convinced that countries like Japan and Great Britain are exploiting the United States economically, much as the United States once exploited Third World nations. Still others are certain that somewhere an absolute paradise has been built and that those who control it are systematically excluding refugees from it. The only section of the country that remotely resembles such a paradise, California, fears that the rest of the country will overrun it. Everywhere, even in California, extremist groups spring up dedicated to anarchy against the government and anyone else who might have had anything to do with the tragedy. A member of one group, the Destructuralists, explains the group's philosophy: "We say that the whole social edifice, from the Boy Scouts right up to the Army, is essentially an addiction, that it is more than unnecessary, it is dangerous. Social structures are the breeding grounds of ideology, greed, and territorialism" (131).

Even among those who cling to hope and work for a better life, the daily thought of inexpressible loss clouds joy. For Strieber it is the knowledge that his mother and brother were incinerated in San Antonio on Warday and that he will eventually develop cancer as a result of his exposure to radiation. Kunetka must face the agonizing doubt that his wife may or may not be dead. For everyone, a world of ease has been obliterated and replaced with a constant struggle for survival. Strieber encapsulates this feeling early in the book: "We are not the people we were on that sharp October day in 1988. . . . Sitting here with my pad and paper, I find that writing about it evokes obscure and powerful feelings. Am I bitter, or angry, or simply sad? So much of what I saw as basic to life is gone; what I counted valuable, worthless" (3).

The power of the work lies in understatement. Just as much of the effectiveness of Solzhenitsyn's *One Day in the Life of Ivan Denisovitch* stems from the fact that it describes what the narrator considers a *good* day in a Soviet prison camp, much of the point of

Warday is made by showing how devastating a relatively minor exchange of nuclear weapons would be. If even a small nuclear war could reduce the level of civilization in this country so drastically, we are left to imagine what an all-out war would do to us.

Warday also deals with the most salient issue raised by the nuclear debate in the 1980s—the Strategic Defense Initiative of the Reagan administration. The Strategic Defense Initiative (SDI) calls for the development of an elaborate, technologically advanced system that would use lasers and particle beam weapons to shoot down Soviet missiles at various stages in their flight. Those who support the system cite as its advantage the fact that it attacks enemy weapons instead of people and does so in such a way that no human being would die even by accident. In addition, they claim, if the system could be perfected, it would, in the words of President Reagan, make nuclear weapons "impotent and obsolete."[30]

A number of objections have been raised against the proposal, however. First is the testimony of many scientists that the complexity of the sort of system the administration proposes would make a completely effective deterrent impossible. The Union of Concerned Scientists sees little hope for the president's dream of a world in which antimissile systems take the place of nuclear weapons:

> No amount of testing under simulated battle conditions could confidently explore the response of a complex defensive system to an actual nuclear attack. In part, this is because the nature of the attack and the attacker's countermeasures, as well as their effectiveness, cannot be known in advance. It is also because one cannot simulate the stress and the demands on the system of the circumstances of war. . . .
>
> Nuclear weapons cannot be made "impotent and obsolete" until, and unless, we have a defense we can trust.[31]

Opponents of nuclear weapons in general have also attacked the system because it could lead to instability in the arms balance and might precipitate war. They reason that, if the United States did attempt to develop an antimissile defense, the Soviets would just produce more missiles in order to overwhelm it. Thus, the defense system would actually serve only to spur the arms race. Opponents argue further that, if the United States actually succeeded in developing a system that could dispose of all Soviet missiles, the Soviets would face a future in which they were open to attack by the United States but could not rely on the old threat of retaliation to deter such an attack. Any attempt by the United States to deploy such an antimissile system could spark a pre-emptive Soviet attack before the system was fully operational.

This scenario causes the nuclear exchange that occurs in *Warday*. The United States begins to deploy the "Spiderweb" antimissile system. The description of this system emphasizes its similarity to Ronald Reagan's SDI: it uses laser weapons launched by missiles to destroy Soviet warheads while they are still in space, and its ultimate goal is to make the United States impervious to any enemy missile attack. The Soviets, too afraid of American technological superiority even to protest the deployment, act in what they consider to be self-defense. They drop nuclear weapons from satellites to set up an EMP effect across the United States. Besides inflicting the terrible damage to the nation's economy that we have already examined, the action gives Kunetka and Strieber an opportunity to distribute evenly the blame for expanding the arms race into the heavens.

While the authors do not dwell excessively on the so-called "Star Wars" issue, it seems to be no coincidence that this fictional warning of the dangers of an SDI-type system came just a year after Reagan's speech announcing a commitment to the SDI concept. It also seems to be no accident that the comments of a fictional former undersecretary of defense about Spiderweb summarize so well the principal objection to such a system: "Although I was not a party to the decision to deploy Spiderweb, I am trying to come to grips with the fact that I was assisting in the management of a system of defense that had drifted into a state of extreme brittleness, in the sense that our own technological superiority was making our enemy increasingly desperate, and thus was actually causing the very war it was intended to prevent" (57).

Given this apparent inability of technology to eliminate the nuclear threat, many people have continued to seek a human solution to the nuclear dilemma. They hope that greater understanding and cooperation between the great powers can deliver the world from the threat of annihilation. In the midst of the Cold War, however, any expectation of such understanding and cooperation seemed nothing more than a pleasant pipe dream.

But the startling changes that the 1990s have brought to East-West relationships have begun to change the climate of the nuclear debate. The rise of *glasnost* and *perestroika*—and the attendant reduction of the Soviet military threat in Europe—has led to levels of cooperation between the United States and Soviet Union not seen since the height of World War II. And as the Soviet threat has, at least temporarily, begun to fade, so too, some feel, has the threat of nuclear holocaust.

The Persian Gulf Crisis of 1990–1991 illustrates the change in the international climate as the world entered the final decade of the century. When the Cold War was at its most frigid, the Iraqi invasion of Kuwait would, no doubt, have provided an occasion for belligerent posturing between East and West, but the threat of nuclear destruction would probably have prevented any overt military action by either the United States or the Soviet Union. Certainly sheer perverse antagonism would have caused the Soviets to veto any effective action by the United Nations Security Council in response to the Iraqi action.

But by the fall of 1990, relations between the Soviet Union and the United States had warmed to such an extent that the Soviets supported a United Nations embargo against Iraq and the deployment of U.S. troops in Saudi Arabia. The image of the Soviet Union joining with the United States and the other nations of the world in a joint action under the banner of the United Nations gave many hope that the nuclear dilemma might at long last be solvable. Indeed, many considered that dilemma already all but solved.

While offering a legitimate source for hope, however, the Persian Gulf Crisis also pointed up the dangers of complacency about nuclear weapons. On the one hand, the urgency of the crisis from an American point of view stemmed, in part, from fears that Iraq was in the process of attempting to develop a nuclear-weapons capacity. The specter of minor third world conflicts escalating into nuclear conflagrations should be a source of genuine concern for anyone concerned with world peace.

Perhaps even more threatening was the widespread speculation that, if war broke out in the Gulf, the United States might retaliate against Iraqi gas attacks with tactical nuclear weapons. For long-term opponents of nuclear war fighting, this speculation seemed depressingly familiar. The danger of theater nuclear war, which just months before had apparently been gasping its last in the forests of Germany, now seemed about to spring back to life in the Arabian sands.

Moreover these developments were occurring in a world that still bristled with nuclear weapons. Despite the warming of East-West relations, neither the United States nor the Soviet Union had begun to move in real terms to reduce its nuclear arsenal. The machinery for worldwide destruction remained firmly in place, and the potential that a limited nuclear exchange could escalate into a general nuclear holocaust, while admittedly reduced, was still very real.

The continuing feeling that all was not quite over as far as the nuclear threat was concerned provided at least part of the emotional thrust of two major films that were released in late 1989 and early 1990. To be sure, *Fatman and Little Boy,* Roland Joffe's account of the development of the atomic bomb, was conceived and produced before the destruction of the Berlin Wall symbolically ended the Cold War and could not take account of the somewhat reduced nuclear threat of the period in which it was released. Still, its attack on the original development of nuclear weapons—and by implication the continued existence of these weapons—provided a reminder of the continued nuclear threat at a time of political euphoria. In much the same way *The Hunt for Red October,* released in the spring of 1990 but carefully set a few years earlier, was set aboard a Soviet nuclear submarine built to provide a mobile launching pad for a devastating offensive strike against the United States. Surely emotional memories of the bad old days of nuclear brinkmanship, combined with the realization that nuclear war was still possible, contributed to the great popularity of the film.

Also in the spring of 1990, a much more direct warning that the world was not yet free of the dangers of nuclear war came in the form of the HBO television film *By Dawn's Early Light.* This latter day *Fail-Safe* is clearly set in a period of unprecedented Soviet-American cooperation, but it details how, even during such a period, a nuclear conflict could occur. It begins with a sobering title: "There are 55,000 nuclear weapons in the world today. Through times of crisis and times of hope, their awesome power has been held in check by the most complex safety system ever devised. A system of machines and men. So far it has not failed."[32] Besides reminding the audience that the nuclear threat is still as potent as ever, the film subtly suggests an equivalence between the current climate of detente and the previous Cold War by noting that the same system that controls nuclear weapons in "times of crisis" controls them in "times of hope."

The film goes on to point out that, however hopeful the times, nuclear destruction is still a threat while nuclear weapons exist. The crisis begins when a missile, apparently fired from an American base in Turkey, is detonated over the Soviet Union and the Soviets respond with an automatic strike against the United States. The American president is shocked by the development since Soviet-American relations "couldn't be better." We soon learn that the original missile was fired by dissident members of the Soviet military who feared the warming of relations between the Soviet Union and the United States and wanted to spark a nuclear war between the two nations. Thus, the film warns that, far from eliminating the threat of nuclear war, the apparently improved world situation could well precipitate one.

The remainder of the film follows a familiar spiral of escalating destruction. Most of the trust that has been built up between the two nations is destroyed by the first blasts of the war. Much of the American military establishment begin to follow their most paranoid instincts in reacting to the crisis. The Chinese, in response to a treaty with the United States, launches their own attack on the Soviet Union. The Soviet response to this attack is mistaken for another attack on the United States, which then launches a larger strike. The virtual destruction of both sides' command structures in these attacks all but eliminates any chance for halting the hostilities. In short, the film provides a thumbnail review of most of the ways that the launching of a single missile could ignite worldwide conflagration.

By raising the specter of nuclear war in an age of—even as a possible result of—Soviet-American rapprochement, *By Dawn's Early Light* brings fictional treatments of the antinuclear debate up to date. Indeed, what we have seen in this brief survey is that an examination of fiction dealing with nuclear war provides an overview of the general movements of that debate during its forty year history. Undoubtedly as new issues emerge, or old ones take renewed prominence, fiction will dramatize them as well, bringing to the attention of a mass audience specific aspects of a debate that might otherwise remain obscure to the public at large.

6
The Dynamic of the Emotional Appeal in Fiction

Of the three types of rhetorical appeal, the emotional is the most obviously compatible with traditional views of the purpose of fiction. Certainly most theories of literary criticism maintain that at least part of the purpose of literature is the stimulation of some kind of pleasure. While the source and the importance of this pleasure varies depending on the theory, the insistence on the pleasurable emotion seems universal.

What rhetorical fiction does is to attempt to use the aesthetic pleasure of the work to help win the reader's allegiance to some thematic point. I have already spoken about the validity of this practice and asserted that, whether or not one agrees that persuasion is a valid purpose of fiction, authors *do* use fiction to persuade. By entering into this persuasive process, fiction facilitates the communication of valuable lessons to mass audiences by leavening the lessons with the aesthetic pleasure.

Thus, a novelist like Samuel Richardson could advance a case for the virtue of chastity in the novel *Pamela*, a form that the pleasure loving masses—who presumably most needed the lesson—would find more attractive than a sermon. Moreover, the novel enhances Richardson's ability to show "virtue rewarded" because it *is* fiction. He did not have to produce a real example of a maidservant who, through her constancy in resisting her master's improper advances, maintained her chastity *and* won the heart and hand of that same gentleman. A moralist or sociologist might have to search far, wide, and long to find such an example in the real world; Richardson had only to look into his own fertile imagination.

Of course, many who have actually read Richardson's novel question how much actual pleasure *Pamela* affords. They argue that it, and other works like it, are heavy-handed and boring and cite this fact to assert that rhetorical fiction is not really literature.

In the light of such attacks, it should be noted that, although the ultimate purpose of rhetorical literature is to make some intellectual point, the work must still deliver the sort of aesthetic pleasure that any other artistic work does. If it does not do so, if the artistic element is so lacking that the audience perceives that the work is simply making a point, it not only forfeits the right to be called literature, it also forfeits the advantages that rhetorical fiction offers. In other words, the whole purpose of couching some intellectual point in a literary work is to make the point more palatable to a mass audience. If the quality which makes it palatable is missing, then the intellectual point will, at best, be only as persuasive in the "fictional" work as it would be in the nonfictional.

Fortunately, proponents of rhetorical fiction can point to many works which have had great success in entertaining audiences. One need look no further than Dickens to see that a truly pleasurable work can instruct its audience. In his time, Dickens attacked abuses in education (*Nicholas Nickleby*), the legal system (*Bleak House*), treatment of the poor (*Oliver Twist*), and the like, all in works whose enduring popularity argue the genuine pleasure they offer. The ongoing validity of the rhetorical approach to fiction can be seen in twentieth-century works as diverse as Upton Sinclair's *The Jungle*, D. H. Lawrence's *Lady Chatterley's Lover*, Evelyn Waugh's *Sword of Honor*, Joseph Heller's *Catch-22*, and Walker Percy's *The Second Coming*, to name a representative few from the ranks of "serious" novels. While we could not reduce the themes of these works to the level of an Aesop's-fable moral, a large part of their purpose is to communicate some point about human life in the hopes of winning or reinforcing the audience's allegiance to that point. At the same time, each work attempts to give the audience the aesthetic pleasure that distinguishes literature from other forms of communication.

The emotional appeal also enters into the study of rhetorical fiction on another level, however. Besides the emotions of aesthetic pleasure, literature will arouse other specific emotions in its audience. Most people feel *something* when they read a book or view a film or play: exultation at the hero's triumph, amusement at the folly of the clown, sadness at the pain of the parted lovers. The dynamic is evident to anyone who has really experienced fiction.

The explanation of the dynamic, however, is not necessarily so evident. After all, when we cheer or laugh or cry at the local cineplex, we are reacting to things that have not actually happened to people who do not actually exist. If we stop and think for a moment about the level of emotional energy we are investing in the unreal, our actions might begin to seem strange. Fortunately for the purveyors of fiction, most people do not stop to examine exactly what they are doing when they react to fiction. But some philosophers and critics do, and a cursory examination of some of their theories may help provide some insight into the use of emotion in rhetorical fiction.

The philosophical problem about emotional responses to fiction centers around the matter of belief. The dilemma is that, while it is understandable for people to experience emotions about things that they believe exist, it seems illogical for them to react to things that they do not believe exist. Colin Radford makes this point most bluntly when he suggests that emotional reactions to fiction are "inconsistent, incoherent and irrational."[1]

Numerous theories have been advanced to deal with this apparent problem, the most famous, perhaps, being Coleridge's dictum about "that willing suspension of disbelief for the moment, which constitutes poetic faith."[2] And while this more or less conscious, if temporary, self-manipulation of our perception of reality has troubled some, it, or something like it, has continued to find adherents to the present day. Eva Schaper, for example, while endeavoring to reject Coleridge's suspension of disbelief, herself develops the concept that we work on two levels of belief when dealing with fiction. On the first level we believe that we are experiencing fiction. On the second level we believe that, in the fiction, things happen to the characters that arouse our emotions.[3] As B. J. Rosebury has pointed out, however, Schaper still fails to explain how we can legitimately react to the nonactual events that are the subjects of level two beliefs.[4] He suggests that Schaper "smuggle[s] the suspension of disbelief back in under a new guise" by implying that at level two we are somehow suppressing the beliefs of level one.[5] Jerry L. Guthrie, on the other hand, confronts the problem of belief head on by insisting that fictional response is a species of self-delusion.[6]

Still attempting to evade the "willing suspension of disbelief," Kendall L. Walton suggests that when we respond to fiction, what we are actually doing is entering into a game in which we pretend that the fictional world shares an actuality with the real world. He asserts, "Tom Sawyer and Willy Loman are neither real nor believed to be. Instead, appreciators are fictional. Rather than somehow promoting fictions to the level of reality, we, as appreciators, descend to the level of fiction."[7] Peter Lamarque sees the dynamic a bit differently, maintaining that when we respond to fiction we allow the fictional characters and events to become psychologically real. "My conclusion then," he says, "is simple: when we respond emotionally to fictional characters we are responding to mental representations of thought-contents identifiable through descriptions derived in suitable ways from the propositional contents of fictional sentences."[8]

Other writers on the matter postulate that when we react emotionally to the fictional we are not so much suspending disbelief as transmuting the fictional into something that we can believe and, therefore, react emotionally to. William Charlton maintains that our emotional response to the fictional is conditional; we essentially say to ourselves that if such a thing were to happen our emotional response would be thus.[9] Barrie Paskin brings up the possibility that when we react to fiction we are relating it to actual cases that parallel the fiction; we are laughing or crying for the real people that we perceive to be in the same situation as the fictional characters.[10] Mark Packer suggests that Aristotle saw tragedy as a representation of an individual case of some universal; our emotional reactions to it are justified by our apprehension that the universal embodied on the stage applies to actual persons in the real world—including ourselves.[11]

Still other critics wonder why any explanation of our reaction to fiction is necessary. They insist, in a variety of ways, that when we react emotionally to fiction, we are actually reacting to fiction, and they don't seem overly worried about the rationality of that reaction. Harold Skulsky suggests that fiction represents for us a "true modal belief,"[12] and John Nolt characterizes reaction to fiction as "modal emotionalism."[13] H. O. Mounce sees absolutely no problem in the fact that we are moved by representations of things that move us in real life.[14] R. T. Allen summarizes this position most eloquently when he says that anyone who needs an explanation of our emotional responses to the fictional "has lost our native and naive delight in stories and story telling, suffers from a lack of imagination and has become drearily prosaic."[15]

Now, if I were a philosopher, I would probably blanche at the number of different—and apparently contradictory—approaches presented here. Being a human being instead, I recognize some merit in each approach. Each suggests to me some truth about how we react when we read a novel or view a drama. I would think that, at least, each represents the results of its author's attempts to examine his or her own reactions to fiction.

Speaking for myself, and a circle of my friends, I know that, in some sense and on some level, our emotional reactions to fiction are, if not irrational, at least nonrational. Nor does this seem strange since emotions themselves, by definition, are not rational. So what we read in a novel or see in a film can—and does—reach through to our emotions as if it were real. It may be that the images and actions the fiction presents bypass some critical function of our reason. Or perhaps we more or less consciously give ourselves over to the work, suppressing our disbelief for the time that we are caught up in the fiction. The precise workings of the inner psychological dynamic is irrelevant to my purpose here. What is important is that fiction does somehow reach us and move us directly.

But we are also capable of an emotional reaction to fiction that depends on a more thoughtful involvement with the work. Often we *do* find some way to relate the characters and events of fiction to real life, whether by treating them as conditionals or by identifying them with actual people including ourselves. Appreciating the plausibility of *Death of a Salesman,* we may pity any actual people who might find themselves in Willy Loman's situation. Identifying similarities between some real person and William Styron's Sophie may help us to feel the agony of her critical choice. Adverting to the fact that when we view *Citizen Kane* we are experiencing a particular—albeit fictional—representation of the vulnerability of idealism to corruption by wealth and power, we may feel legitimate sorrow knowing how universal that vulnerability is.

And if we look at the major methods that fiction uses to reach the emotions of its audience, we can see how it relies on all these dynamics to work. For example, our most direct emotional responses occur when we encounter powerfully vivid images. The sight of a starving child holding an empty bowl, a piercing scream of pain or terror, the aroma of a field of flowers after a rain are all capable of arousing immediate emotion. We generally do not need to think before feeling pity or fear or joy when confronted with such images. We simply respond. This fact explains why advertising companies search for the right set of images for magazine and television advertisements, and it accounts for corporations' spending millions of dollars to develop logos for their companies. And, according to Mounce, it explains the power of fiction: "The roots of art are the same as those of magic. They lie in our primitive reactions to images."[16]

The imagery of nuclear war, of course, can be particularly vivid. Photographs or descriptions of people horribly burned by the heat wave or suffering the violently debilitating stages of fatal radiation sickness can evoke powerful feelings of pity. John Hersey's *Hiroshima* engenders strong antinuclear feelings in its audience, not by moralizing about the destructiveness of the bomb, but by describing in detail the effect of the bombing on ordinary people who had little or no part in Japan's war effort. One image from the book has stayed with me ever since I first read it as a high school sophomore. Hersey describes a priest taking refuge in a park crowded with wounded after the bombing. Responding to a cry for water, he comes upon a horrifying sight: "When he had penetrated the bushes, he saw there were about twenty men, and they were all in exactly the same nightmarish state: their faces were wholly burned, their eyesockets were hollow, the fluid from their melted eyes had run down their cheeks. (They must have had their faces upturned when the bomb went off; perhaps they were anti-aircraft personnel.) Their mouths were mere swollen, pus-covered wounds, which they could not bear to stretch enough to admit the spout of the teapot."[17] This single image, more than anything else in the book, brought home to me on an emotional level the horrors of nuclear war. It made real and palpable a danger that had previously been abstract.

While actual images of real victims can evoke extremely powerful emotions, however, they do have certain disadvantages. They may arouse intense pity in the audience, but they may also, or alternatively, arouse other passions less conducive to the writer's purpose. An American confronted with images of Hiroshima victims may begin to feel guilty that his nation had caused such suffering. In itself, of course, such guilt could be as effective as pity in generating revulsion for nuclear weapons. But when we get beyond the immediate reaction to the realm where our emotions are mediated by thought, we may want to resist the guilt. In the present instance, that resistance could spawn a reactive justification of the bombing. The American reader, even while admitting that the suffering he sees is pitiable, may be inclined to salve his sense of guilt by citing the bombing of Pearl Harbor as a justification for the destruction of Hiroshima and Nagasaki.

One tactic documentary sources have used to try to circumvent this problem is to link the image of destruction to the audience itself. *If You Love This Planet* finds a very subtle way to accomplish this. The film is a record of a lecture given by Helen Caldicott to a group of college students dealing, in part, with the effects of nuclear weapons on the population of Hiroshima and Nagasaki.

As she talks, images of the wounded Japanese, mainly women and children, appear on the screen. In order to make a psychological connection between these actual victims and Americans as potential victims, the filmmakers intercut these images with reaction shots of the audience. An image of a young Japanese woman whose face is horribly burned, for example, is immediately followed by a close-up of a fresh-faced, blond co-ed listening to the lecture. The juxtaposition of the two images may work only subconsciously, but it makes the point that this lovely young woman could suffer the same fate as her Japanese counterpart.

If we accept this principle that most people will respond more powerfully to images with which they can identify, then the most effective way of arousing an American audience's emotions would actually be to show the effect of nuclear war on the United States, rather than just to hint at it subliminally as *If You Love This Planet* does. And, in fact, many nonfiction sources do attempt to do this. Countless works try to make the concept of a nuclear blast vividly understandable for an American audience by describing the effects of a nuclear bomb detonated directly over the Empire State Building—or some other landmark—drawing concentric circles to show what various effects of the blast would be at different distances from Ground Zero. In making their points this way, the authors of nonfiction have actually entered the fictional realm. They are dealing, not with actual images drawn from the real world, but with invented images. The images may be realistic in that they are accurate projections drawn from known scientific fact, but they still exist only in the realm of the imagination—the realm of the fictional.

Of course, the sort of fictional images one is likely to find in a predominantly documentary work will be tentative and crude. The victims they present will be drawn in the most shadowy outlines. In short, the limited fiction that documentary writers are able to employ will generally lack the power of traditional literary fiction to draw the audience into close identification with the characters and therefore engage its emotions on the highest level. Here the writer of fiction has an advantage over the writer of nonfiction. If the fiction writer can create his characters vividly enough to make us feel that we know them—or at least people like them—then the images he creates of their suffering may have nearly the same emotional effect on us that the actual suffering of real people would. And the more like us those characters seem, the greater our emotional response will be. In the case of nuclear war, novels and films can confront us with images of Americans like us being subjected to the horrors of nuclear war and bring about the desired emotional response even though no such attack on the United States has ever occurred.

Consequently, antinuclear fiction has offered its readers a range of images to arouse an emotional commitment to the cause of nuclear disarmament. *Level 7* ends with a vision of the last man on Earth straining against the terminal effects of radiation poisoning to turn on his music speaker so he will not die in silence. The most effective moments of *Triumph* are descriptions, without Wylie's editorial comments, of the breakdown of social order in the wake of a nuclear attack: masses trampling each other to death in a race for shelter, ordinarily law-abiding citizens shooting down their neighbors to protect their own supplies, mobs of scavengers running down and raping a terrified lone woman. Aural imagery can also be used to great effect: the screech emitted by melted telephones at the end of the film *Fail-Safe* is powerfully unnerving in its implications. In *On the Beach* the beeping of a radio sending unit in California at first suggests hope, then strikes an ironic note of disillusionment when it is discovered to be the action of the wind rather than a human being. At the end of the film, it provides the sound track accompaniment to otherwise silent shots of the lifeless streets of Melbourne, heightening our sense of utter desolation by underlining the fact that no one is left alive to answer its call.

Besides being the product of powerful images, emotions can be evoked by the situations the authors create for their characters. And once again, we may respond directly to the situation presented in the work. This point is made by John Nolt in speaking about Wordsworth's "She Dwelt Among the Untrodden Ways": "The poem is sad not because of sad associations but because it represents a situation—the death of a lover—which makes us sad directly."[18] At the same time—or alternatively, depending on the audience—we may be moved because we relate the situation in the fiction to real life.

The basic situation Shute deals with in *On the Beach*, for example, inherently begs the reader's pity: the world has suffered a nuclear holocaust and the population of the Southern Hemisphere—represented by a group living in Melbourne—is waiting for the inevitable arrival of lethal radioactive fallout. Given this situation, Shute's characters must find some way of bringing meaning to lives that have no future. Faced with this representation, we can pity the characters themselves or we can pity real people—in this case the whole human race—who might face this or a similar situation.

Unsurprisingly, antinuclear fiction frequently uses the postapocalyptic situation to try to make nuclear destruction emotionally real to its audience. In *Level 7*, Roshwald, like Shute, puts his characters into a situation over which they have no control and which robs their lives of any purpose. In the end, they too must grimly face inevitable death as a result of nuclear war. Other life-after-the-bomb situations are less hopeless but can be equally evocative emotionally. *Ape and Essence*, for example, horrifies the reader with a world in which deformed babies are routinely and impassively sacrificed to Satan as a form of genetic engineering. We have already seen that *Riddley Walker* takes place in a depressingly primitive and savage world thousands of years in the future.

In addition to the postapocalyptic situation, antinuclear fiction also employs the nuclear-crisis situation, in which people attempt to control forces that threaten to explode into war. The most famous of such works are *Fail-Safe* and *Dr. Strangelove*, in which characters must race against time to prevent renegade aircraft from precipitating World War III. Other works depict attempts to prevent nuclear holocaust on a less immediate, but more philosophical level. *A Canticle for Leibowitz* locates the real source of the nuclear nightmare in the fallen nature of man and places its main characters—several generations of monks—in the situation of attempting to convince various influential people that the only hope for man's survival lies in transforming his relationship with his technology. The intensity of these situations is powerful enough to sweep us up into an uncritical concern for the characters themselves. But such an immediate response does not prevent us subsequently from reflecting on the fact that, in our own small ways, we share their dilemma—we, too, feel the anxiety and frustration of trying to prevent nuclear war.

The same dynamic applies when we move to the power of a work's plot to evoke strong emotion. As with image and situation, our response to plot may be largely visceral, that is, we may find ourselves on the edge of our seat with excitement or weeping with sadness just because we have become so involved in the action of the story. But, more reflectively, we may see the action presented as one that could befall ourselves or someone we know, and our emotional reaction may be to some extent based on this level of identification.

In *Fail-Safe,* for example, Burdick and Wheeler manipulate the reader's emotions through the basic action of the novel: the efforts of the president and his advisers to prevent a nuclear tragedy. The stakes here—the possible destruction of civilization—are such that our emotional involvement should be engaged. But to increase and personalize this emotional engagement, the authors provide us with the characters of General Black and his wife. Because a nuclear war would mean the destruction of New York, where the Blacks live, and Washington, where General Black is attending a meeting, these two attractive characters are directly threatened by the potential disaster.

Thus, the book presents us with a suspense plot in which characters with whom we identify work against time and circumstance to save their own lives and those of their loved ones. Every movement of the plot involves some ultimately unsuccessful plan to resolve the crisis peacefully. At each turn our hopes are raised, along with those of the characters, only to be dashed. Each episode increases in emotional pitch until a final hysterical plea by the bomber pilot's wife fails to deter him in his mission. The final plot movement, of course, plays directly on the identification that has been developed between the reader and the Blacks. In order to prevent a general holocaust, the president must order Black to drop the bomb on New York City. We are relieved that the conflict in the novel has been resolved successfully: a general holocaust has been averted. But overriding this relief will be our horror that the two people with whom we most identify have been destroyed. Presumably, this sense of combined horror and loss is the emotional reaction that Burdick and Wheeler are aiming for.

In our examination of the techniques used by fiction to arouse emotions, we have been moving up the ladder of abstraction. Images, which probably provide the greatest stimulant for the audience's immediate emotional reaction, are also the most concrete. Situation and plot retain some of the concreteness of image, but begin to move toward a more conceptual level—a level that invites more reflection and, therefore, an even greater potential for audience identification with the fictional. When we move to the level of theme, we move to the most abstract, conceptual level of all, and, I believe, a level where emotional involvement is most heavily based on linking the fiction to reality.

Here we are most clearly dealing with the dynamic that Mark Packer talks about in "The Conditions of Aesthetic Feeling in Aristotle's Poetics." In delineating Aristotle's view of how tragedy works, Packer notes, "Pity, then is the result of a judgement concerning the possession by the tragic character of certain general moral features, and fear is conditioned by the realization that these general moral qualities are attributable to oneself as well."[19] I would push the realm of this dynamic to include all emotional responses to any kind of rhetorical fiction, and apply the same general principle to the audience's perception of theme in the work. When we recognize the truth of a powerful universal statement, we will feel some emotion, especially to the extent that we recognize the relevance of that statement to our own lives.

This is especially true of the statements that antinuclear fiction makes. When we recognize the theme of *A Canticle for Leibowitz*—that nuclear weapons are an ineradicable expression of mankind's capacity for evil—we may well feel a profound sense of fear. Much the same can be said of our reactions when we accept *Warday*'s contention that even a limited nuclear war would effectively destroy this country or *Fail-Safe*'s insistence on the very real probability of accidental nuclear war. In all these cases, indeed in all cases of rhetorical fiction, thematic evocation of emotional response necessarily depends on our linking the work to the real world. We feel emotion precisely because we realize the work is telling us a truth about the world that exists beyond itself—the world in which we actually live.

But the relationships we draw between fiction and the real world enter into the rhetorical use of emotion in another way. For if the fiction is to succeed as a rhetorical act, we must be encouraged to transfer the emotions we feel for the work to the real world problem that the work is portraying. The mixture of horror and hope that we feel at the end of *Fail-Safe*, for example, will be rhetorically useless if we look only to the past—if the emotions have reference only to the fictional event that we have just experienced. The success of the book is dependent on our putting the emotional experience in real context by acknowledging the universal truths that the events in the book portray. Only then will our emotions actually help to accomplish the change in attitude that rhetorical fiction aims at.

In this respect, a particular scene in the novel is significant. Just before Moscow is destroyed, the Soviet premier makes a promise to the president: "I am willing to come to the United States and to agree to disarmament. Before I leave I will take steps that will make it impossible for our armed forces to repeat what has happened today" (277). After agreeing to the premier's visit and promising to take the same precautionary steps, the president notes that the incident provides a warning of future dangers: "We damn well better learn carefully from it. More and more of our lives will be determined by these computer systems. . . . They represent a new kind of power—despotism even—and we've got to learn how to constitutionalize it" (279–80).

This conversation does nothing to influence the major action of the book; all the decisions that will determine the denouement have already been made. The passage is important, however, in that it signals to the audience that something remains to be done in the real world after the fictional events are completed. It provides a direction in which we are to channel our emotional reaction and suggests that we should be supporting some action to solve the nuclear crisis. Here, in fact, the authors provide us with specific actions we should support: rejection of mechanized systems of defense and eventual total disarmament. By introducing these possible actions at the moment that the emotional pitch is greatest—immediately before the bombings of Moscow and New York—Burdick and Wheeler hope to use our emotional reaction to motivate our support for these solutions.

Nor is *Fail-Safe* unique in using this strategy. The plot developments of many works serve to channel the emotional effect of the audience. The act of sending a community of monks to serve the extraterrestrial colonies at the end of *A Canticle for Leibowitz* emphasizes the need for man to confront his flawed nature. In the same vein, Martin Eliot's rejection of his career as a nuclear physicist challenges the audience to act on the emotions that the novel *The New Men* has aroused. At the end of *Warday*, Strieber prays that mankind might gain wisdom from the fictional fire that he and Kunetka have invented in their novel. In all of these cases, the authors use some pointer to channel the emotional reactions that the work arouses.

The importance of thus directing the audience's emotional reactions stems from the fact that the emotional appeal is very powerful but also volatile. The rational appeal sets out its point as clearly and attractively as it can, directly soliciting the audience's assent. The emotional appeal, as we have seen, presents images, situations, and actions to provoke a certain reaction in the audience. Even if the correct emotional reaction is provoked in us, however, we may not embrace the course of action that the author advocates. An image of the effects of nuclear war may frighten us, but our fear may cause us to support an increase in the nuclear arsenal rather than the decrease that the author may have had in mind.

This danger of confusion—the threat that the emotions raised by a work will take on a life of their own which might counteract the rhetorical purpose of the author—explains why many fiction writers, in addition to placing "signposts" in the plot to channel our emotions, tie the emotional appeal to a strong statement of theme. We have seen that *Fail-Safe* inserts a thematic statement just before the emotional climax of the novel in order to channel the emotional reaction toward a support of nuclear disarmament. A similar tactic is taken in the film of *On the Beach*. The final shots show the empty streets of Melbourne after all life has been destroyed, the director's purpose being to frighten us into an opposition to nuclear weapons. There is a danger, however, that we will be so devastated by the images that we will believe any attempt to reduce the nuclear danger to be futile. In such a case, the emotional effect of the film would be at odds with the rhetorical purpose. In order to prevent a fatalistic reaction, Stanley Kramer ends the film with a close-up of a banner which reads, "There is still time, brother."

While the phenomenon of the author's supplying a thematic statement to accompany the emotional climax of the work is not universal in the fiction of nuclear war, it does occur frequently. The highly emotional climactic scene in *Wargames* ends with an image of the computer display screen bearing the message, "The only winning move is not to play." In the midst of his bittersweet tour of his old home in New York, *Warday*'s Strieber reflects on the theme of personal responsibility that permeates the novel: "The land was not despoiled by chemical companies, nor the war caused by countries. It was us, each one. We are all accountable for our era" (339–40). As Abbot Zerchi dies from wounds received in a nuclear blast at the climax of *A Canticle for Leibowitz*, his thoughts summarize Miller's theme: "He did not ask *why* God would raise up a creature of primal innocence from the shoulder of Mrs. Grales, or why God gave to it the preternatural gifts of Eden—those gifts which Man had been trying to seize by brute force again from Heaven since first he lost them. He had seen primal innocence in those eyes, and a promise of resurrection" (311–12).

As I have said, all of these statements are designed to help channel the movement of the reader's emotions. At the same time, however, the emotions give force to the thematic statements. Caught up in the emotion of the scene in particular or the work as a whole, we may feel more impelled to accept and act on the message that the work is presenting. And this effect is the power of rhetorical fiction. Because literature works so much on an emotional level, and because emotion can influence a person's actions so greatly, fiction provides a dynamic springboard for whatever message the author wishes to convey.

7

The Emotions of Antinuclear Fiction

In the last chapter, I alluded to the emotions of pity and fear as central components of the classical definition of tragedy. Perhaps not so coincidentally, these are two of the most potently persuasive emotions that antinuclear fiction employs. In the *Rhetoric* Aristotle defines pity as "a sense of pain at what we take to be an evil of a destructive or painful kind, which befalls one who does not deserve it, which we think we ourselves or some one allied to us might likewise suffer, and when this possibility seems near at hand."[1] His definition of fear is very similar: "Fear may be defined as a pain or disturbance arising from a mental image of impending evil of a destructive or painful sort."[2] In fact Aristotle admits that the origins of the two emotions are often the same and that what really distinguishes them is the perceived victim of the evil: "Speaking generally, we may say that those things make us fear which, when they befall, or threaten, others, make us pity."[3] Thus, a young person in sound health will be moved to pity when someone suffers a heart attack because he does not perceive such a danger as being an immediate threat to him. An older person, on the other hand, may feel fear in addition to pity, recognizing that he himself may be vulnerable to a heart attack as well.

Although this sense of imminence, or potential imminence, seemed to be the crucial factor in arousing either pity or fear as far as Aristotle was concerned, I suspect that the nature of the threat may also be a factor. We do seem to be more likely to respond with fear to a danger that is very violent or highly unusual and with pity to a danger that may ultimately be as damaging but which seems less violent or more common. While we may feel pity when Willy Loman commits suicide, for example, we may feel fear in addition to pity when we read about the unusually violent death of Joe Christmas in William Faulkner's *Light in August*.

In any case, the two emotions are obviously very close and can be experienced simultaneously. Whether a particular member of the audience of a work experiences pity or fear or both when confronted with representations of a certain kind of danger will frequently depend on the sort of emotional potential he brings to the work rather than on anything the author does. Consequently distinguishing between works that arouse pity and those that arouse fear must be, to some extent, arbitrary and may say more about the emotional makeup of whoever is making the distinctions than about the actual intentions of the authors. Nevertheless, we can be sure that both the emotions are used in antinuclear fiction even if we disagree about which emotion is being raised in any particular example.

Nonfiction works that attack nuclear war find the means to arouse the audience's pity readily at hand. As we have already pointed out, numerous documentaries graphically depict the results of the bombings of Hiroshima and Nagasaki: people scarred with burns from the intense heat wave, people sickened and dying from the effects of radiation poisoning, people suffering from various radiation-induced cancers. The images of these victims in photographs or in films—or in their stories told in books like John Hersey's *Hiroshima* or Peter Wyden's *Day One*—tend to evoke empathy in sensitive people. In the absence of any specific antipathy, normal men and women seem to have a natural revulsion toward seeing their fellow human beings in pain. True, this revulsion may express itself passively in efforts to avoid encountering suffering, but at its most noble, this revulsion can generate a positive desire to help end the victim's pain.

Spurred by this sort of desire, people contribute to movements to ease world hunger, cure disease, and aid victims of natural disasters. On a deeper level, a person's empathy with the victims of a tragedy may cause him to seek to remove the root causes of the tragedy. Since the root causes of the suffering at Hiroshima and Nagasaki were the atomic explosions and since those explosions can no longer be prevented, the sympathetic audience may transfer their pity to potential sufferers of future blasts. By doing so, they would become more disposed to the principle of nuclear disarmament.

This dynamic, of course, is as effective in fiction as it is in nonfiction. In fact, fiction may provide an even greater potential for arousing pity since its goal is to create a world so vivid and so plausible that the reader can lose himself in it, accepting it as its own reality. To this end, the fiction writer can explore the personalities and thoughts of his characters as fully as he sees fit. The nonfiction writer, on the other hand, is at the mercy of his subjects' desire for privacy. Moreover, the documentarist is bound by reality—by what actually exists in the world. The fiction writer is free to create any possibility.

And so a novelist like Nevil Shute in *On the Beach* can carefully select a cross section of especially sympathetic characters to follow through humanity's final days. One set of characters consists of a married couple, Peter Holmes and his wife Mary, who have just become the parents of a baby girl. They are young, attractive, and dedicated to each other. In other circumstances, their lives would be the ideal of domestic bliss. But we—and they—know that they are not going to be able to fulfill the potential of that domestic ideal. They will not grow old together. They will not have another child. They will not even be allowed to see the one they have grow up. They will, instead, be forced to choose between killing her and watching her die a horrible death from radiation poisoning. The pity that such a situation immediately arouses may be increased by the fact that the wife is unable to accept the inevitability of death, continually denying reality whenever anyone brings up the subject of radiation. Our reaction may be that she should not *have* to accept such a reality.

The second couple that Shute focuses on are the American submarine commander, Dwight Towers, and the Australian play-girl, Moira Davidson. In making one of his characters an American, Shute attempts to ensure the empathy of a large part of his audience, readers in the United States. Moreover, Towers is almost an archetypal American hero—a paragon of right-thinking and devotion to duty. He possesses all of the qualities that leaders in fictional works are supposed to possess—all of the qualities that usually enable them to defeat any antagonist they might face. Unfortunately, no one, not even a man with the heroic attributes of Dwight Towers, can affect the outcome of this novel. No human action can prevent the lethal radioactive cloud from descending. Part of the pity that we feel for Towers stems from our recognition of the helplessness he feels as a man of action who is powerless to act effectively. In the film made from the novel, Gregory Peck delivers a speech that makes Towers's sense of helplessness explicit: "You see, in the Navy during the war, I got used to the idea that something might happen to me, that I might not make it. And I also got used to the idea that my wife and children were safe at home. They'd be all right no matter what. What I didn't reckon with was that in this—this kind of monstrous war, something might happen to them and not to me. Well, it did, and I can't—I can't cope with it." The fact that he also cannot help

Moira Davidson—the surrogate for his wife—increases the poignancy of his situation.

Moira is another stock character from fiction: the charming wastrel with the heart of gold who is waiting for the right person or set of circumstances to reform her. Literature is filled with examples, from Prince Hal to Scarlett O'Hara, which indicate that this archetype somehow strikes a responsive emotional chord in audiences. In Moira's case, the potential savior is Dwight Towers, who needs the only thing she has left to give—her love. For a while, it seems that they will find some kind of fulfillment, but, in the end she cannot make Towers forget the memory of his wife and children: "If she had had more time things might have been different, but it would have taken many years. Five years, at least, she thought, until the memories of Sharon and of Junior and of Helen had begun to fade; then he would have turned to her, and she could have given him another family and made him happy again. Five years were not granted to her; it would be five days, more likely" (244). Once again, our pity for the character arises from our appreciation of her lost potential. In any other conventional fiction, Moira *would* be granted the time to complete her reformation, bringing happiness both to herself and to Towers. As with the other characters, however, the forces that stand in the way of this fulfillment are out of her control. Nuclear death—inevitable, impersonal, and undeserved—robs her of a happy ending.

The final object of pity in *On the Beach* is the scientist, John Osborne. He, too, is an example of the reprobate: a charming but cynical alcoholic. The alcoholism, however, is softened by the fact that it stems from his guilt over being a scientist in the wake of the world's greatest scientific disaster. In a way, he feels responsible for the war and is willing to admit that responsibility, but, at the same time, he is a victim of it: he will suffer the same penalty as everyone else. Unlike the scientists in other films of the fifties, he will discover no great solution to the dilemma; the single hope that science offers here, the Jorgensen effect, proves to be an illusion. Moreover he will face his fate alone; he has no companion with whom to share what remains of his life. He is in love with Moira but must sublimate his feelings because of her love for Towers. Once again, the film makes Osborne's isolation clear. In an attempt to comfort Peter Holmes, he speaks of his own loneliness: "I envy you. . . . You have someone to worry about. I never envied anyone before; I never really believed in it. But you,

yes, I do. I envy you. You have a wife, child, nappies to change.
You have a lot to remember. You're fortunate to have someone to
worry about. There are those who don't you know. . . . We let it
all go by the board. It's too late now. But you. You've had it all."

One might argue that Shute is being manipulative in choosing
these particular characters to represent dying humanity. Where
are the thieves, rapists, and murderers? Instead of caring, sensitive military men who are more victims of the war than per-
petrators, why doesn't Shute examine the militarists who remain
adamant about the necessity of the terrible destruction in order to
halt the Red Menace or the tentacles of capitalist imperialism? In
short, we may wonder where the underside of humanity is in
these last days of the species. There is little or no reference to that
underside in either the book or the film. People go about their
daily lives—in almost all cases productive, useful lives—awaiting
the end with stiff upper lips. We hear no mention of mass panics
or looting, see no evidence that the human race would face its
certain end with anything less than dignity and discipline.

Some might dismiss this view of human nature as unrealistic.
Even if the majority accepted extinction with the equanimity that
Shute's characters do, most readers would have difficulty believing that everyone would. The history of disaster tells us that a
certain percentage of people *do* panic in such circumstances.
Others *do* attempt to exploit the situation through looting and
other crimes. Certainly we would not expect everyone who ordinarily lived on the far side of the law to reform when faced with
death. To the extent that *On the Beach* ignores these human characteristics, it is unrealistic.

This criticism, however, ignores the rhetorical strategy of the
work. Shute intends to persuade by securing, to the highest
degree possible, the audience's sympathy for his characters.
Showing the various levels of perfidy that humanity might be
capable of in the event of a nuclear war would be counterproduc-
tive in a work that attempts to arouse the sympathy of the human
race for itself. By demonstrating that nuclear war would extinguish a species that could produce the admirable family unit of
the Holmeses, the possibility for unselfish love shown by Towers
and Moira, and the intellectual potential of a scientist like Osborne, Shute is suggesting the parameters of the waste that such a
war would cause.

Numerous other works of antinuclear fiction, of course, also
employ pity. The film *Testament*, for example, brings the victims of
nuclear tragedy physically closer to home for American audiences

by dramatizing the death of the residents of a small California town. While it is true that *Testament* may be a bit more realistic than *On the Beach* in that the pressures of facing death do tend to unravel the central family's stoicism somewhat, director Lynne Littman, on the whole, is using the same strategy that Shute does. The sympathetic depiction of the final days of humanity in Mordecai Roshwald's novel *Level 7* also appeals to the reader's pity as do the final chapters of *A Canticle for Leibowitz*, in which Abbot Zerchi must deal with a mother and baby who are both dying of radiation sickness.

While pity plays a part in the emotional appeal of Nicholas Meyer's television film, *The Day After*, fear seems much more crucial to its rhetorical strategy. Meyer begins by insuring the maximum level of identification for an American audience through his choice of setting: Lawrence, Kansas, almost the exact center of the nation. To enhance this identification, Meyer superimposes the opening credits on a montage of day-to-day life in Lawrence and the surrounding areas. Farmers harvest corn in the nearby fields; children play in a park; workers in a milk plant run their bottling machines; students go to classes at the university. Knowing that we are viewing the opening of a film about nuclear holocaust, we realize that these are meant to be glimpses of the lives of people like us—lives that are about to be destroyed by a calamity that threatens us daily. Through this identification, Meyer is conditioning us to feel the sense of imminent danger that fear demands.

To increase this sense of imminent danger, Meyer develops the crisis that leads to the holocaust, not in direct confrontations between great leaders in the corridors of power, but obliquely on the screens of ubiquitous television sets. As an audience, we receive the same information that the people in the film receive at the same time that they receive it and in the same way. Meyer's mode of exposition, then, heightens our identification with the characters in the film.

In order to hold as many mirrors as possible up to the members of his audience, Meyer presents a number of reactions that ordinary people might feel as a nuclear crisis evolves. Dr. Oakes and his wife deny the reality that they see unfolding on their television screens, taking comfort in having seen the Cuban Missile Crisis resolved peacefully. Mrs. Dahlberg and her daughter Denise are too involved in the mundane details of their daily lives to realize the seriousness of their situation. Joe Huxley, the college professor, recognizes the danger but, realizing his helplessness in the nuclear age, takes refuge in flip cynicism to mask his terror. Mr. Dahlberg, the farmer, must confront reality when it intrudes into his world of marriage plans and baseball games, forcing him to worry about what he, as the head of a family, can do to protect his loved ones when the danger comes.

Having set up the identifications that will provide the groundwork for fear, Meyer attempts to exploit the repertoire of nuclear dangers by showing their effects on these people. First, in a series of special effects shots that last for nearly four minutes, he tries to give some idea of the initial effects of the attack. Those in downtown Kansas City are incinerated. Included among them is Dr. Oakes's daughter. We see her vaporized as she runs from a shelter, her flesh disintegrating to reveal a skeleton that glows red briefly and then disappears. Meyer works the same effect on a number of other people, including a few groups of children. He also shows us the blast effects on buildings, apparently in an attempt to overawe us with the force of the weapons. Buildings fly apart, glass shatters and showers into the streets, a metal bridge is torn from its foundation. Intercut with these special-effects shots are actual films of bomb tests showing buildings flattened by the shock wave and great fir trees bending almost flat and even breaking.

But this four minute sequence only begins Meyer's assault on the viewer's emotions. True to the facts of nuclear war—and Meyer is scrupulous in making sure that his depiction is accurate—the survivors of the missile strikes face an ongoing struggle for life. One of the most obvious and immediate problems that they must deal with is the breakdown of the technology that modern man depends on in his daily life. As a result of the EMP effect, electrical systems have been disrupted. We have already seen some of the results of the effect during the attack: electronic ignitions in cars fail causing a massive traffic jam among those attempting to evacuate; the lights in an operating room go out in the middle of surgery; a fountain in the city dies as the electrical pump that fed it fails. Only after the attack, however, is the effect explained and its implications made clear. During a meeting of the doctors at the Lawrence University Hospital, someone asks why they cannot generate enough power to pump water. Another doctor answers him: "When a large nuclear device is airburst at a high altitude, a lot of electrical disruption can be created, principally with radios, communication systems, electrical wires, computers, cars, transistors. Of course, it's all theoretical. It's never happened before. In short, very little electricity."

The implication is obvious: civilization, as dependent as it is on electronic technology, will not survive even the most personally harmless effects of nuclear war. We are left to imagine how many will die because the medical equipment has failed. We are also largely left to imagine the other effects in society of this breakdown of technology. At night city streets will be lit, if at all, by the uncertain glow of fires. Police cars, like all other equipment relying on electronic components, will be rendered useless. Refrigeration will cease, and food will spoil. Even water supplies will be limited by the failure of electrical pumps.

Paralleling this breakdown in technology—indeed, to some extent caused by it—is the breakdown of social order. For years books and films have painted bizarre and terrifying pictures of the social anarchy that would follow nuclear war—or that audiences fear would follow it. Novels like *A Canticle for Leibowitz* and *Riddley Walker* suggest a social collapse so extensive that the effects would be felt for generations. Films like *Panic in the Year Zero* and the various "Mad Max" movies immerse their characters in this terrifying anarchy. As I have already mentioned, Philip Wylie, in *Triumph*, presents vivid images of the complete breakdown of social order that might follow a nuclear holocaust.

By comparison with many of these portrayals, *The Day After* is restrained. A doctor tells Oakes that people are storming the hospital demanding to be cared for. A rumor is reported that soldiers are shooting people for looting, rape, and other crimes. Near the end of the film, Dr. Oakes sees a man about to be executed, although neither he nor we know what crime the man has committed. In three scenes, however, Meyer shows the breakdown of order more vividly and, therefore, more frighteningly. In one, a crowd of hungry people attacks soldiers who are rationing food to them from the back of a truck. Even though the soldiers fire several shots into the crowd, the people overwhelm them, and we assume that the soldiers have been beaten to death. In another scene, a group of thirsty survivors line up at a water spigot and take turns drinking. They methodically chase one man away from the water, however. Although their reasons remain unexplained, they seem to be united in the cause of keeping this one man from the water. Finally, someone carrying a revolver appears and forces the crowd to give the man water. The implication is clear: in a postapocalyptic world, those with strength—or with weapons—will rule.

The final example of social anarchy is the most telling. Dahlberg rides home from a meeting of farmers to discover a crowd of

drifters on his land butchering one of his cattle. Angered, he
confronts the group with his rifle in hand. As he nears the
people, however, he sees that many of them are women and
children, and his mood shifts from anger to pity. Instead of
shooting, he protests plaintively, "This is my home." At that
moment, someone shoots him in the back with a shotgun, and
Meyer cuts to a scene of his wife and young daughter, hearing the
sound without realizing what has happened. The incident encapsulates both the horror and the pity of the breakdown of civilization.

The most basic source of fear in the latter part of *The Day After*,
however, is radioactivity. Even more than the unprecedented
power of the blasts themselves, the threat of radiation poisoning
represents for many the unique danger of nuclear weapons. One
of the principal reasons for this deep fear is the sense of mystery
that surrounds radiation. It is an unknown force capable of striking terror in the same way that a new disease might. When
confronted with the threat of radiation, people conjure up all sorts
of strange images ranging from the very real threat of cancer to
more questionable speculation about gross mutations.

As I have already pointed out in an earlier chapter, many
science fiction films of the 1950s exploited the fear of radiation for
sensational effect. Visions of giant scorpions, giant ants, and giant
housewives—all given their freakish character through contact
with radiation—piqued the juvenile fears of countless Saturday
matinee moviegoers. We can well imagine the subconscious effect
of *The Incredible Shrinking Man*, for example, on its audience of pre-
teenagers as they watch a grown man shrink to the size of a
microbe after passing through a cloud of radiation. Although the
character in the film finds some comfort at the end in a philosophical acceptance of the relativity of size and the thought that "To
God there is no zero," we can assume that the normal twelve-
year-old boy would much rather grow up to be an NBA hopeful
than down to be the family cat's snack. Of course, as we have
already noted, these conceptions are ridiculous. Certainly, radiation *can* cause mutations in organisms, but these mutations most
commonly affect generations subsequent to those receiving the
radiation and would not take the dramatic forms shown in these
films. As Strieber and Kunetka point out in *Warday*, the mutations
would probably be more mundane: an increase in the various
kinds of birth defects with which we are already all too familiar.

It might be unwise to dismiss these films too quickly, however.
True, even the young people sitting in the theaters probably did

not take their premises too seriously. Very few of the children who saw *Them!* actually expected to see a giant ant crawl out of their city's sewer systems. They were content to experience the same sort of thrill that an amusement part ride offers—a fleeting sense of imaginary danger. What is interesting is the vehicle chosen to arouse that thrill. Attempts to provoke fright in an audience often play on actual, deep-seated psychological fears. They succeed because the palpable, but often unrealistic, "horror" presented on screen represents and evokes the very real anxieties lodged deep in the psyche.

In an article entitled "Reflections on Horror Movies," Robert Brustein suggests an equivalence between the supernatural dangers that provided the foundation for the terror of many early horror stories—including many of the great 1930s horror films— and the scientific dangers that stood at the root of the terror in the science fiction films of the 1950s. *Dracula, The Mummy,* and *The Wolf Man* presented threats that audiences found mysterious and frightening because they had their source in the occult—an unexplored world that man could not reach or influence on his own. But to the average American of the 1950s, science was as remote, as unreachable, and at least as dangerous as the world of vampires and mummies. Nuclear radiation was certainly one of the most provocative of the dangers that science had introduced: an invisible, uncontrollable power that somehow threatened man's existence. Thus, these films, as ridiculous as they are, may say much about the level of psychological fear that radiation engendered in Americans during the period.

Along these lines it may be no coincidence that in so many of these films radiation somehow changes the size of man relative to his world. In *Them!*, for example, common ants become threatening because they grow beyond man's power to control them. In *The Incredible Shrinking Man,* the effect of radiation is to make the hero shrink progressively throughout the film so that a spider that he would ordinarily ignore or step on becomes a dangerous monster he must engage in deadly combat. Again, on a conscious level, these stories are designed to frighten children momentarily and to show off what were then state-of-the-art special effects techniques. I don't think we would go too far wrong, however, in inferring that the premises of the films play upon man's sense that his stature *had* somehow changed since he had begun to tamper with the atom. In unleashing the destructive capacity of this invisible particle, man *had* lost control over his environment. The smallest thing in his universe—the atom—*had* become larger than him—*had* threatened to extinguish him. Of course, the realization of such a possible subtext to these films might have been beyond the grasp of their youthful audiences and beyond the notice of adults who, for the most part, scorned the genre entirely. But the deep-seated psychological fear of radiation—a fear that children *did* live with daily during the period—might well have contributed to their emotions while watching the films.

In any case, there is ample evidence that the fear of radiation is a powerful one, even when it is treated more plausibly. In fact, when Miller raises the specter of genetic mutation in *A Canticle for Leibowitz*, he may succeed in arousing our fears more than the makers of *Them!* do because we may actually feel that such mutation could be a real result of nuclear war. Although his casual mention of extra limbs and fingers may not have the immediately terrifying effect of the sight of a hungry giant ant, the concept that an unseen force can play havoc with our reproduction systems does frighten the thoughtful reader on a very basic level. Much the same point can be made about Hoban's *Riddley Walker*. Indeed, his description of the deformed Eusa folk far outstrips anything in Miller—or in 1950s science fiction—in its capacity to frighten us: "Faces like bad dreams. Faces with 3 eyes and no nose. Faces with 1 eye and a snout. Humps on back and hans growing out of shoulders wer the leas of it they had every kynd of crookitness and ther shapes and shadders wivvering and wayvering on the wall with the shadder of Goodparley twissing and terning" (174).

Given the time span of the film, *The Day After* must confine itself to depicting the more immediate effects of exposure to radiation. However, the fact that these effects may be less spectacular than genetic mutation does not mean that they are not frightening. In one scene, Dahlberg's daughter cannot bear being in the family's basement fallout shelter and bolts outside to cavort in fields that are covered with radioactive ash. The young medical student who goes out to bring her back delivers a short speech that cuts to the core of our fear of radiation: "You can't see it. You can't feel it. And you can't taste it. But it's here, right now, all around us. It's going through you like an X-ray. Right into your cells. What do you think killed all these animals?" By emphasizing the invisibility and deadliness of radiation Meyer taps into the audience's primal fears. And the presentation of the girl's deterioration throughout the remainder of the film exploits those fears. Her hair thins, and she develops a deathly pallor. Later, the pallor is explained: a blood stain on the front of her dress near the vagina tells us that she is hemorrhaging. Because of massive casualties from the blast, however, nothing can be done for her even after she is taken to the hospital: she is placed in a hospice—actually the local gym—to await death with hundreds of other terminal patients.

The same fate awaits other characters. Caught in the open at the time of the blast, Doctor Oakes also has received a fatal dose of radiation. As the film progresses, he grows pale and bald, develops sores, and eventually collapses only to awaken in the same hospice. Although he recovers temporarily, it is clear at the end that he, too, will soon die. A soldier who was caught in the open by the blast alludes to the problems of diarrhea and nausea that are the earliest symptoms of radiation sickness. We last see him in the hospice, screaming in pain and suffering hallucinations.

Although these immediate effects are the ones most thoroughly explored in the film, there are allusions, if only by implication, to other kinds of danger. One of the characters in the film is a pregnant woman whom we first see being wheeled into the hospital two weeks before her baby is due, apparently on the verge of premature delivery. We next see her, still pregnant, a few weeks after the bomb has gone off. Although no one mentions the dangers of genetic malformation, the very presence of a pregnant woman will call to the viewer's mind the effects of radiation on reproduction. While the exposure may have occurred too late in this particular woman's pregnancy to cause any malformation in the baby about to be delivered, it has had an opportunity to affect the mother in terms of future pregnancy and ultimately to affect her child's own reproductive organs.

Thus, *The Day After* does attempt to exploit most of the fears of the nuclear age. By using the word "exploit," however, I do not mean to imply any negative connotation. Meyer does not sensationalize the dangers. Indeed, he presents the various horrors of nuclear war tastefully, perhaps in deference to the film's presence on prime-time network television. A crawl at the end of the film, in fact, admits that the effects of nuclear war would probably be worse than Meyer portrays them. This reluctance to draw the picture as vividly as possible, however, may ultimately damage his efforts to strike real terror in his audience. In an article in *American Film* magazine, French film director Marcel Ophuls evaluates those moments of the film that are designed to be most horrifying—the scenes of actual destruction:

On the whole, however, the special effects of *The Day After,* the earnest, well-meaning efforts to make us taste and feel the violence of nuclear catastrophe seem woefully inadequate, naive, and almost clumsy. Some of the shots of the actual explosion appear to be archival footage from Los Alamos and Bikini, tinted pink and run through a series of chemical baths. Others are miniature models or unconvincing tricks to make human figures change color before disintegrating in the nuclear blast.[5]

Such judgments are subjective, of course, and many people seem to have been genuinely moved by the film, although, as Ophuls also suggests, many may have been moved more by the idea of *The Day After* than by its execution. Nevertheless, the film remains the most widely experienced single fictional effort to acquaint the public at large with the various horrors of nuclear war.

The emotions of pity and fear have reference to the victims of nuclear destruction. It is also possible, however, to arouse emotions against the proponents of nuclear war. To do so, the author of the work will attack the ethical appeal of those who support the development and deployment of nuclear weapons in order to discredit their position. This procedure is known in logic, of course, as the fallacy of the argument *ad hominem*. The fact that the technique is unsound according to the rules of logic, however, does not make it any less effective as a persuasive device. Moreover, as we shall see, the attacks on the people in the works we will be studying are frequently so closely tied to the issues at hand that the onus of the logical flaw is muted. In any case, the primary negative emotions that antinuclear fiction attempts to arouse are anger and scorn.

Most works of antinuclear fiction that attempt to arouse anger against the proponents of nuclear weapons do not target specific individuals or even groups. Instead they direct their anger at a nameless, faceless "they" who are somehow responsible for the nuclear problem. For example, near the end of the film *Testament*, frustration builds up in Carol Wetherly to such an extent that she falls down on her knees and, in what amounts to an inverted prayer, damns all those responsible for the destruction. Since we have been conditioned to identify with this character, we are being invited to share her anger at those responsible, even though we are unable to identify those people specifically.

The same dynamic applies to *Level 7*. Once again, besides pity for the characters we know—particularly X-127—we also are prodded to feel anger at the leaders who have engineered the end of the human race. No doubt this anger begins when the authorities trick the main characters into descending to Level 7 without revealing that they will have to remain there forever. Later in the book, we learn how cynical the leaders are about human priorities. The relatively safe shelter levels of 4, 5, and 6 are all reserved for an elite of little more than half a million people, including the very leaders who are responsible for the nuclear predicament. The masses will inhabit levels 1 and 2, which are insufficient to protect them from an all-out war or to sustain them if the surface of the Earth remains radioactive for a prolonged period. The policy immediately strikes the reader— and X-127—as self-serving and undemocratic and generates resentment against the leadership presented in the novel. Certainly, we can sympathize with the anger that X-127 feels in the wake of the nuclear war. At one point he reflects on the leaders' reluctance to tell the shelter dwellers how long the surface of the Earth will remain radioactive:

> If we could contact them, those leaders of ours, we would get the truth pretty soon. There are ways of squeezing it out of men without using atomic bombs. . . .
> My guess is that the truth is worse than many people think. Otherwise our leaders would tell us all they knew. But they do not, perhaps because they are ashamed. Or maybe they are repentant.
> To hell with them, anyway! (115–16)

This sort of nonspecific antipathy makes perfect sense in a work dealing with nuclear weapons. One of the principal frustrations of the nuclear problem is that it is so complex we cannot blame it entirely on any one individual or nation. Most objective chroniclers of the nuclear age, from Bertrand Russell to Freeman Dyson, seem to agree that no one side of the arms race is totally responsible for the buildup of weapons. Even while they have been adding to their nuclear stockpiles throughout the past forty years, the officials of both the United States and the Soviet Union have consistently denounced nuclear weapons in general. Given the potential danger that the weapons present to their nations— not to mention the actual ongoing expense of the arms race—we can assume that these denunciations are sincere, at least in part. Unfortunately these nations have become trapped in the spiral of nuclear expansion, victims of burgeoning scientific breakthroughs and lingering human fear.

And if we cannot point the finger of blame at any nation, how much more difficult is it to accuse particular individuals who have served those nations? Strieber and Kunetka introduce this problem in *Warday*. During their travels, the authors meet a Canadian who expresses great anger toward Americans in general for the devastation that has affected his country. While we may not share his anger, we may reflect on our own responsibility when he asks if Americans ever thought about the impact of the war on their neighbors. The question personalizes the issue; after all, we live in a democratic country and choose the leaders who control that country's policies. Must we not share the responsibility for the actions that country takes? Of course, we realize that the complexity of the nation and the world makes such anger directed at an individual citizen unreasonable. The same principle should tell us that it is also dubious to lay the blame for the nuclear predicament at the feet of any individual or group of individuals.

Nevertheless, a few works *do* attempt to identify specific targets for the reader's anger. *Fail-Safe*, for example, treats most of its characters sympathetically, including the generals in charge of the nation's nuclear weapons. One character, however, emerges as a clear-cut villain: the civilian analyst Groteschele. From his first appearance, Groteschele evokes ominous feelings in General Black. When we later receive a full view of Groteschele's philosophy, we see that Black's uneasiness is well founded. We learn that Groteschele first became famous for a dissertation advocating that the United States adopt a first-strike policy in regard to nuclear weapons. Because Americans like to think of themselves as peace-loving people who fight only when they or their allies are directly attacked, we should find Groteschele's philosophy especially repugnant. In fact, one of the generals in the film angrily denounces Groteschele's advice, comparing it to the thinking that went into the Japanese attack on Pearl Harbor, which, for Americans, remains an archetypal act of international perfidy.

Little in Groteschele's personality mitigates this repugnance. While we learn that much of his ambition and ruthlessness is the result of his being the son of a Jewish refugee from the Nazi holocaust, the ruthlessness soon becomes unappetizing. Significantly, we learn that during World War II, Groteschele worked for Army Intelligence interrogating captured SS officers. In reaction to these prisoners' remarks about "rabbit-like" Jews, Groteschele embarked on what may seem an unhealthy course of action to outdo them in toughness, adopting a regimen of exercise that left him as "physically tough as the SS troopers, his belly as flat, his face as expressionless" (107). Groteschele's fashioning himself in the likeness of the SS troopers suggests a kind of equivalence between the Nazis and himself. Thus, he is linked with the primary symbol of evil in our time, a factor that increases his villainy in our eyes. Moreover, Groteschele's tendency to mimic his enemy also operates in his approach to the Soviet Union. After all, he advocates a first-strike policy—the kind of policy that he warns the Soviet Union is capable of. Here, too, he takes on the qualities of his enemy—an enemy that many in Burdick and Wheeler's audience would consider a near equivalent of Nazi Germany.

Finally, we are bound to be repulsed further when we learn the hidden motivations of Groteschele's actions. His initial advocacy of the first-strike policy stems from the fact that it is a controversial issue, which, if handled properly, can make him famous quickly. Later, as we observe Groteschele's tryst with a woman named Evelyn Wolfe, we learn other personal motives for his fascination with nuclear weapons: "It was not he, Groteschele, the physical man, who was attractive to women. It was Groteschele, the magic man, the man who understood the universe, the man who knew how and when the buttons would be pushed" (121–22). Even if we did not already hate Groteschele, the glee that he takes in planning the destruction of the world—and the perverted sexual drive that underlies the glee—would certainly provoke our rage against him at this point.

It is interesting to note that Groteschele seems to have had definite counterparts in the real world. *Fail-Safe* does pattern many of its characters on real people: the description of the president unmistakably links him to John Kennedy; the Soviet premier actually *is* Nikita Khrushchev. Groteschele seems to reflect many actual civilian analysts of the early 1960s, most notably Herman Kahn and Henry Kissinger. In fact, Burdick and Wheeler speak of him as a forerunner of these men. Like Kissinger, Groteschele is affiliated with a "prestigious Eastern university" and rose to fame with a book expounding unorthodox views of nuclear war. Like Kahn, Groteschele advocates the use of nuclear weapons under certain circumstances. Also like Kahn, Groteschele has a rather flip wit about the subject of nuclear war. Finally both Groteschele and Kahn speak of "Doomsday Devices." Whether Kahn and Kissinger shared some of Groteschele's personal qualities is problematical and probably irrelevant. In arousing anger against Groteschele, the authors hope to make the reader reject not only Kahn and Kissinger, but the whole class of civilian analysts and their theories of strike and counterstrike, graduated nuclear war, acceptable losses, and so forth. To do so they have struck at the most famous members of the class, employing a particularly repulsive character to do so. It should be noted that the care they take to establish Groteschele's resemblance to his enemy of the moment implies that his enemy—the Soviets—have their own detestable analysts who echo Groteschele's own blithe talk about the art of nuclear war.

The other emotion that antinuclear writers have evoked against the proponents of nuclear war is scorn, the functional emotion of satire. Walter M. Miller employs mild scorn in his treatment of Thon Taddeo Pfardentrott in *A Canticle for Leibowitz*. As the representative of science, Thon Taddeo holds a pivotal position, and our attitude toward him will help shape our reaction to the divorce of science from morality that Miller's novel attacks. The Thon is a condescending genius, the Francis Bacon of his age, but his self-pride and arrogance frequently seem ridiculous when Miller emphasizes that his level of scientific knowledge is primitive when compared to that of our own age. At one point he is astounded—and visibly jealous—when he discovers that one of the monks, using the ancient documents preserved in the abbey, has succeeded in reinventing the electric light. Hoban uses a similar technique in *Riddley Walker*. His image of Goodparley—as technologically ignorant as the rest of the characters in the book—searching for the secret of atomic power is meant to strike us as ridiculous.

The antinuclear work that employs scorn to the greatest effect, however, is Stanley Kubrick's *Dr. Strangelove*. Virtually no character, and, therefore, no class of people connected with nuclear weapons, escapes Kubrick's satire. The cast is filled with people who march toward nuclear destruction, each to the beat of his own demented drummer: the mad general obsessed with a Communist plot to fluoridate the water, the bomber commander ready to do nuclear combat "toe to toe with the Russkies," the Pentagon general who recommends a full-scale strike against the Soviet Union promising American casualties of only "twenty million, give or take, depending on the breaks," the determinedly bland United States president who chastises people for fighting in the war room, the ex-Nazi civilian analyst whose eyes light up at the thought of being locked in a mine shaft with thousands of beautiful women for the next ninety-three years. Each embodies the contradictions and absurdities that Kubrick sees at every level of the nuclear-weapons establishment.

The central satiric strategy of the film is to show what a potently disastrous combination paranoia and patriotism can be. No one in the cast—at least no one in a position of authority—seems immune from the destructive mixture. Most obviously affected is General Jack D. Ripper, the certifiable maniac who opens the film by ordering his command to attack the Soviet Union. Skillfully underplayed by Sterling Hayden, the character could, at first, be taken as a serious portrait of an obsessed military man. We begin to see how laughably mad he really is only when he begins to explain the reasons for his actions: "I can no longer sit back and allow Communist infiltration, Communist indoctrination, Communist subversion, and the international Communist conspiracy to sap and impurify all of our precious bodily fluids." The opening of this speech is meant to recall the sorts of things politicians and military leaders actually did say during the height of the Communist witch-hunts of the 1950s. It links Ripper with those who continued to see Communist conspiracy everywhere, even in 1964 after the witch-hunts themselves had largely died out. The customary language of such people leads us to expect Ripper to speak of the sapping and impurifying of "our free and independent spirit" or "our American way of life." Instead we hear the completely unexpected and apparently literal reference to "precious bodily fluids." The audience may have heard the Communist conspiracy linked to many things, but probably not to bodily fluids. Given the distance between bodily fluids and the various other things that Communist conspiracies might attack—the economic system, personal freedoms, even morality—we might share Buck Turgidsen's puzzlement about what the reference means. On the other hand, we may simply leap to the conclusion that Merkin Muffley draws—that Ripper is out of his mind.

This second reaction is vindicated when Ripper explains how the Communists are threatening the bodily fluids of all loyal Americans—through the fluoridation of water. We discover, here, that Ripper is one of the last holdouts in a controversy that had ended years before the film was made. At the time that communities first began fluoridating their drinking water in 1946, some people actually did feel uneasy about the process. A dramatic decrease in the number of cavities in children born after the process began coupled with the lack of any evidence of harmful effects from fluoridation, however, ended most opposition. By 1964, the whole question of fluoridating water had become nothing more than an amusing footnote in recent cultural history. Ripper's continuing to make a point of the controversy and seeing a Communist plot in it instantly marks him as paranoid and colors everything else he says and does with a hue of absurdity.

Unfortunately for the world, Ripper's paranoia is inextricably linked to his patriotism. If he cared only about himself, he could maintain his own safety, drinking grain alcohol and rain water and depriving women of his essence, without bothering to strike at the root of the Soviet threat that has made these precautions necessary. But Ripper is a loyal American who takes seriously his duty to protect his country from any threat, even if he has to disobey orders to do so. At one point he tells Mandrake that the Communists are even contaminating ice cream. "Ice cream, Mandrake! Children's ice cream!" Here we have an image of the world that Ripper is fighting for—a defenseless child eating an ice cream cone. The image is naively—even pathetically—sentimental, but its influence has put the security of the world in jeopardy.

Ripper is not the only paranoid military man in the film, however. In fact, based on what we see here, paranoia would seem to be a requirement, if not for induction into the armed forces, at least for promotion. Consider the minor character of Bat Guano, who is willing to allow the world to be destroyed rather than trust his fellow man. When Mandrake pleads with him to be allowed to contact the president with the code that will recall the bombers, Guano's initial reaction is to arrest him. Unaware of what is going on at the base, Guano is not sure whom to trust, and, unconsciously echoing Ripper's earlier orders, decides to trust no one. His distrust extends particularly to Group Captain Mandrake who, while an ally, wears a different uniform.

Here, again, Guano's paranoia is linked to patriotism, and the shallowness of this patriotism is emphasized by his homage to that most archetypal of American corporations, the Coca Cola Company. When Mandrake orders him to shoot the lock off a Coke machine for the change to make a phone call to the president, Guano hesitates at first, citing the fact that the machine is private property. He eventually succumbs to Mandrake's insistence, but delivers a warning that remains one of the most remembered lines in the film: "Okay. I'm going to get your money for you. But if you don't get the President of the United States on that phone, you know what's going to happen to you? You're going to have to answer to the Coca Cola Company." Like Ripper, Guano's actions are controlled by a mindless allegiance to the shallowest concept of the American way of life. He would rather see the world go up in flames than damage one of the country's primary icons. The way the scene is played and filmed—right down to the slapstick ending in which the Coke machine sprays

Guano in the face—heaps scorn on the character and the attitude he caricatures.

General Buck Turgidsen, the Pentagon general played by George C. Scott, shows us how this combination of runaway paranoia and patriotism affects decisions at the highest level of the military establishment. In the midst of a crisis that demands the most delicate and open negotiations, Turgidsen is horrified at the thought that the Soviet ambassador will be allowed into the war room. In an effort to have the ambassador expelled, he attempts to plant a camera on him and alleges that the ambassador was trying to photograph "the big board." It is also Turgidsen who raises the possibility that the runaway bomber "might be some sort of Commie trick." His continual references to the "Commie menace" and his willingness to sacrifice millions of lives in order to destroy this menace also suggest the levels to which his patriotism has become debased by his paranoia. For him, patriotism has lost its emphasis on love of country and protection of values and has become an excuse to hate and destroy someone else.

Paranoia even infects such an apparently normal character as President Merkin Muffley. On the surface, at least, Muffley seems calm and rational. Indeed, in his conversations with Turgidsen, the two are perfect foils. He is outraged by the fact that Ripper could launch such a strike and strongly condemns Turgidsen's suggestion that the United States commit itself to a full-scale attack. His faults seem to be largely those of ineffectuality; he does not really seem to be in control of events for which he is ultimately responsible. But he *has* been affected, if not afflicted, by the rampant paranoia of the nuclear age. He has, after all, approved Plan R, which enables a line commander to authorize a nuclear strike in the event that the Soviet Union killed the president in a sneak attack. It is, of course, this plan that Ripper uses to launch his attack. Thus, the crisis was made possible by a policy that arose from the same type of paranoia that Turgidsen exemplifies. To the extent that Muffley administers the policies that this paranoia dictates, he is responsible for the disaster.

In a way, Dr. Strangelove may be the most paranoid person in the film. The whole system of strategic planning which he represents is founded on paranoia—on attempting to imagine the worst thing that the enemy can do. Moreover, it aims at arousing and exploiting the enemy's fear. Strangelove admits as much when he explains the theory of the Doomsday Machine to Muffley: "Deterrence is the art of producing in the mind of the enemy the fear to attack." He completes the deadly mix between paranoia and patriotism by expressing the most perverted sense of loyalty in the film. Despite a rather condescending attitude toward the Chief Executive, Strangelove seems devoted to his president. Unfortunately, the level of this devotion is conditioned by memories of his Nazi past. He frequently forgets himself, calling Muffley "Mein Fuehrer." Evidently, his loyalty is more to an ideal of authoritarianism—an authoritarianism that relies heavily on his advice—than to the principles on which the United States is founded.

Kubrick suggests, moreover, that paranoia is not limited to the American side of the nuclear arms race. Near the end of the film, we see that, true to Buck Turgidsen's fears, the Soviet ambassador *does* have a camera and *is* photographing the big board. The fact that he does so after it is clear that Major Kong's plane will succeed in bombing its target underlines the uselessness and absurdity of the action. The implication is that the Soviet ambassador has been so indoctrinated with distrust that he instinctively gathers as much secret information as he can, even though the world is on the verge of destruction while he does so. The very existence of a Soviet Doomsday Machine indicates that this paranoia is carried through to the highest levels of the Soviet command.

A second important strategy that Kubrick uses to generate scorn for his characters is the introduction of sexual elements in a manner and a context that suggests a close relationship between sex and war. For example, Ripper reveals that he discovered the Russian fluoridation plot after experiencing problems with his sexual potency. We realize that Ripper has experienced a sexual problem that any man, particularly a man of his age in a high-pressure occupation, might feel. Instead of recognizing his human limitations, however, Ripper invents a Russian plot that blends easily with the sort of paranoia he has been trained to indulge as a member of the military establishment.

The effect of this confession on the audience is complex. First of all, we are amused by the realization that he is substituting the absurd Russian plot for a quite rational explanation of a personal problem. In this respect, our amusement is justified by the sort of self-deception involved in his denial mechanism. On a less noble, even a nasty level, we may also be amused by the nature of Ripper's problem. Any sort of physical disability or dysfunction is a potential source of amusement for others. This aspect of the human character may not be edifying, but we cannot ignore it.

Moreover, any sexual disability or dysfunction is often seen as particularly funny. Thus, the very fact that Ripper is experiencing a sexual problem is capable of amusing many members of the audience on a very basic—even base—level. This amusement may be increased by the fact that Ripper, as an Air Force general, is a representative of a particularly macho occupation. The viewer may justify his laughter by pointing to the fact that he is really amused by the hypocrisy of the virile posturing that hides the sexual impotence, but that explanation does not disguise the fact that the humor the viewer feels in this instance would be cruel if Ripper were a real human being.

In any case, any cruelty that the humor might contain is probably offset by the fact that Ripper uses war as a substitute for sex, and, therefore, involves the rest of the world in his problem. This connection between sex and war is communicated more or less subliminally in Ripper's case, but within the general context of the film, the connection is clear.

Ripper has two strategies for resisting the Soviet takeover of the United States. First, he abstains from sex, and thereby protects his own purity of essence. Second, he launches a preemptive strike against the Soviet Union, the force that is fluoridating the water and disturbing the essence of other Americans. Logically, of course, these two actions have no connection, but in Ripper's unbalanced mind, sexual maneuvering and nuclear strategy are parallel aspects of the same battle. Continuing this subliminal connection between war and sex is Ripper's reference to the soldiers under his command as his boys. At one point he tells Mandrake that they are like children to him. In fact, they seem to be the only children he has, the offspring of his marriage to the United States Air Force. When they finally surrender to their own troops, Ripper's sense of betrayal is that of a man abandoned to his enemies by his own sons. And Kubrick may be providing a visual sign of Ripper's equation of war with sex by having the character occasionally wield his machine gun at groin level as if it were a large phallus.

This phallic imagery appears in both of the other main settings of the film. William Bayer has pointed out that when Major Kong takes his ride on the bomb at the end of the film, he sits astride it, and it stretches out from his groin like a giant penis.[6] In the war room, the phallic symbol takes the form of Dr. Strangelove's recalcitrant arm. Throughout the film, whenever the ex-Nazi scientific advisor is excited, his arm, apparently of its own volition, rises in a Nazi salute while the doctor tries to beat it back down.

As his excitement increases, the arm becomes more unruly. While this bit of business is an obvious reminder that many of the scientists who helped develop nuclear weapons and the missile systems to deliver them had worked for the Nazis, it is also suggestive of the action of the penis during sexual arousal. Since Strangelove's arm rises more often as the crisis deepens, Kubrick may be suggesting that nuclear war is a kind of aphrodisiac for the doctor, or at least for that part of him that has learned to love the bomb.

Of course, talking about phallic symbols in any work is dangerous. We run the risk of seeing veiled sexual images in any object that could even remotely suggest one. Indeed, I would be hesitant to suggest the symbols I have if Kubrick did not imply an equation between war and sexuality so constantly and so insistently. For example, we first meet Buck Turgidsen in his bedroom where the news of Ripper's insubordination interrupts a liaison with his secretary. He then must replace sex with war by going to the Pentagon instead of carrying through with his sexual encounter. In order to reinforce the substitution of war for sex, Kubrick has Turgidsen tell his secretary, "Begin your countdown and Old Bucky'll be back before you can say 'Blast off!' " In making this statement, Turgidsen is using the language of missile warfare to communicate a sexual message. In fact, we might see his desire to launch an all-out strike against the Soviet Union as a sublimated effort to find sexual release after being called away from his mistress.

Such sexual references pervade the film. While the sexual component of Major Kong's last ride is communicated symbolically, his first appearance is explicitly linked to sex. When we first see him, he is enjoying *Playboy* magazine, and the importance of this detail is argued by the fact that Kubrick lingers on it. He gives us an establishing shot of Kong holding the magazine, and then cuts to a shot from Kong's perspective showing that he is looking at the centerfold. Significantly, the girl in the centerfold is posed almost exactly as Turgidsen's secretary was when we first saw her. Also, if we look closely at a later scene, we can see that Turgidsen has the same magazine in the War Room. Kubrick seems to be making an effort to link the sexual interests of the two men, perhaps indicating that those who carry out Turgidsen's orders respond to the same motivation that he does.

We find more evidence of this theory when Kong orders the men to check the contents of their survival packages. Included in the list he reads off are silk stockings, lipstick, and prophylactics.

While the audience may still be speculating on the usefulness of these items for survival purposes, Kong points out that "a fella could have a pretty good weekend in Vegas with all that stuff." He seems, here, to be sharing Turgidsen's perception of an underlying relationship between sex and war. Finally, even Colonel Bat Guano, a soldier's soldier who would not think of going into battle with loose change in his pockets, expresses an underlying obsession with sex. The best explanation he can think of for the battle over Burpelson Air Force Base is that Mandrake was leading a mutiny of "deviated preverts." In short, the military men in the film seem to be obsessed with sex.

As was true with the paranoid patriotism, this sexual obsession finds a home in the highest level of civilian authority as well as in the military. Besides betraying vague clues to an unorthodox sexual chemistry with the involuntary erections of his arm, Strangelove expresses a more direct kind of sexual interest when it becomes clear that the Doomsday Machine really will go off. As a means of continuing civilization, he proposes that certain carefully selected American leaders be sent down mine shafts to breed a new generation of free people. He envisions a ratio of ten women to every man: "I hasten to add that since the men will be required to do prodigious service along these lines, the women will have to be selected for their sexual characteristics, which will have to be of a highly stimulating nature." Clearly we have the makings here of an adolescent boy's paradise: ten beautiful women to each man, and the only work the man has to do is have sex with them. Nice work if you can get it.

We might have suspected Strangelove's sexual interest. Given the symbolic equivalence between war and sex, his status as a nuclear-war analyst suggests that he is obsessed with sexual thoughts. The involuntary erections of his arm are a visual manifestation of this preoccupation. We may, however, be surprised at the readiness with which Merkin Muffley becomes intrigued by the idea. Muffley, who seems about as asexual a character as we are likely to meet, also lights up at the ten-to-one ration. Even he, who seems to be the soul of dignity, yearns to run wild under a world devastated by nuclear destruction. Just as war is a substitute for a vanished potency for Ripper, an alternate means of sexual indulgence for Turgidsen, and a means of escaping repression for Strangelove, it represents an awakening for Muffley who has been resisting it all along.

Again, as was true with paranoid patriotism, sexual obsession is not limited to the Americans in the film. When Muffley initially has difficulty contacting the Soviet premier, the Soviet ambassador explains that "Our Premier is a man of the people, but he is also a man, if you follow my meaning," and gives Muffley another number to try. The loud music that Muffley hears on the other end of the phone suggests that the premier, like Turgidsen, has been caught in the middle of a liaison. Later, the ambassador praises Strangelove's mine shaft idea. The fact that this praise immediately follows the statement about choosing women for their highly stimulating sexual characteristics reveals what portion of the plan the ambassador is most taken with.

Partially, Kubrick introduces this sexual component to make the characters seem even more ridiculous than they already are—to heighten the *ad hominem* attack. Since certain references to sex are seen as inherently funny, linking these references to the characters undercuts their ethical appeal and makes us tend to laugh at everything they say, including what they say about nuclear war. Since these comments, as we have seen in a previous chapter, parallel actual arguments of nuclear proponents, our scorn for the fictional characters and their attitudes may transfer to their real life counterparts and their statements.

On another level, however, Kubrick may be suggesting some underlying psychological causes for the arms race. There is a body of responsible opinion that would see an involvement in nuclear war—or any war—as a subconscious sexual expression. Certainly Caldicott, who entitled one of her books *Missile Envy* in obvious reference to the psychological term "penis envy," accepts this view:

> These hideous weapons of killing and mass genocide may be a symptom of several male emotions: inadequate sexuality and a need to continually prove their virility plus a primitive fascination with killing. I recently watched a filmed launching of an MX missile. It rose slowly out of the ground, surrounded by smoke and flames and elongated into the air—it was indeed a very sexual sight, and when armed with the ten warheads it will explode with the most almighty orgasm. The names the military uses are laden with psychosexual overtones: missile erector, thrust-to-weight ratio, soft lay down, deep penetration, hard line and soft line.[7]

Whether one chooses to accept this view of the dynamic of war or not, Kubrick *does* seem to be suggesting such a connection in *Dr. Strangelove*. It quickly becomes clear that everyone involved in the crisis is an overgrown adolescent, using war as a substitute for sex. As our appreciation of this point grows, all the talk about keeping the world safe for democracy and the necessity of meeting threat with counterthreat, falls ever more hollowly on the ear. We realize that these noble expressions are mere smokescreens for a motive that, if expressed, would seem ridiculous.

The final major emotion that antinuclear fiction attempts to arouse—hope—may seem out of place in the company of the various negative emotions we have been discussing. The psychological makeup of mankind, however, makes it necessary for hope to walk hand in hand with fear, anger, and the rest. Helen Caldicott speaks of the phenomenon of psychic numbing in relation to nuclear war, pointing out that, faced with the extinction of the species, people deny the danger by ignoring it. The purpose of the antinuclear works that we have been discussing is to break through that strategy of denial and confront people with the dangers. We have seen some of the emotions fiction writers attempt to arouse in order to break through this inertia. However, the goal of creating opposition to nuclear war will be lost if, in breaking through this barrier of denial, the fiction creates a sense of hopelessness—a sense that nothing anyone does can avert the terrible destruction of nuclear war.

And so it seems necessary to leave the audience with some feeling of hope, some sense that effective action is possible. *Fail-Safe* ends on a strong statement of belief in man's ability to rid the world of the danger that he has brought into it. *The Day After* attempts to instill hope by showing the pregnant woman ultimately accepting the possibility of life by having her baby. Even works like *A Canticle for Leibowitz* and *Riddley Walker*, which suggest that the occurrence of a nuclear war would not finally end the nuclear threat, find some measure of hope. In *Canticle*, the monks never stop fighting the destructive tendencies of mankind, even following the remnants of the human race into space in order to preach their gospel. Although the end of *Riddley Walker* makes it clear that man will continue his search for destructive power, Riddley himself rejects the search and dedicates himself to a life as a storyteller, warning his audience repeatedly about the dangers of "the 1 Big 1."

Some works are more problematical, however. At the end of the novel *On the Beach*, for example, all of the main characters either have died of radiation poisoning or have committed suicide. We seem to be left with an utterly hopeless view of the end of the human race in a nuclear war. The same is true of *Level 7*, and here the final days of mankind are unrelieved by any sense of beauty or romance: the human race dies like an animal trapped in a burrow.

Even more stark is *Dr. Strangelove*. The final images are of the Doomsday Machine bombs exploding while the tune "We'll Meet Again" plays on the sound track. We can either assume that everyone on Earth will die of radiation poisoning, or, if some are lucky enough to find shelter, their descendants will emerge in ninety-three years to renew the conflict. Moreover, Kubrick robs us of any chance to feel sentimental about the demise of our species. He regards the destruction as a great cosmic joke—a bitter joke, perhaps, but a joke nonetheless. There seems to be little room in these works for hope.

The hope in these cases may be dependent, not on specific signals in the works themselves, but on mankind's natural instinct to demand survival. As we read X-127's final words, we may believe nuclear weapons actually *will* destroy civilization in the end. The montage of explosions at the end of *Strangelove* may convince us that Kubrick himself sees little hope that the world can solve its nuclear problem. We may experience a moment of despair, accepting these dire predictions for our future. But mankind's instinct for survival is persistent. Whatever our intellectual convictions, that instinct will force us to seek some sense of hope. We may take comfort in the fact that the destruction portrayed in these works has not yet occurred and, therefore, may be prevented. We may even react strongly to the apparently hopeless attitudes of the makers of the works—for example, grow angry with Kubrick for the glib fatalism that he seems to adopt in *Strangelove*. In such a case our anger may be transformed into a determination to prove him wrong.

On the other hand, we may perceive that the creators of these works have looked at the facts and have refused to abandon hope themselves: in the very act of making these rhetorical fictions, they have expressed some hope that something *can* still be done to prevent the end of civilization. We realize that they have helped us imagine the complete destruction of our world, not to frighten us into submission to the nuclear menace, but to give us a taste of the disaster that such war would certainly bring. In doing so, we realize, they intend to move us to positive action. And it is in this positive action that the real hope for mankind is generated.

The film made of *On the Beach* makes this concept explicit. The novel ends with Moira Davidson, the last principal character left alive, taking her lethal pill. The book, therefore, ends on the apparently despairing note that we have been discussing. As readers, we must supply hope with our reactive drive for survival. The film, however, delivers the underlying message of all these works overtly. After a scene showing Moira taking her pill, the film cuts to shots of the deserted streets of Melbourne. Here, Stanley Kramer is simply providing a visual equivalent for the destruction of the human race. The last shot, however, makes the point that ultimately all antinuclear fiction makes by closing in on a banner that had graced a Salvation Army revival. Literally, the sign refers to the possibility of human repentance from sin, but, in terms of nuclear war, it also speaks to us from an imagined future about the possibilities of our troubled present: "There is still time, brother!"

8

Threads: A Synthesis

Up to this point, I have been discussing the three modes of appeal in isolation from one another. While this approach has been helpful in maintaining a certain degree of clarity, it may give the impression that the modes work more or less independently. Actually, however, they do not. In any real work that entertains any hope of success, the three modes of rhetorical appeal collaborate to bring about the desired effect.

Aristotle himself makes this point: "Now Rhetoric finds its end in judgment—for the audience judges the counsels that are given, and the decision of the jury is a judgment; and hence the speaker must not merely see to it that his speech shall be convincing and persuasive, but he must give the right impression of himself, and get his judge into the right state of mind."[1] True, in any given work, one or two of the modes may dominate, but the speaker or writer will always present some impression of character, will always make some kind of case for his proposition, and will always leave the audience with some emotion.

Fiction is, of course, not exempt from this dynamic, as an examination of the BBC film *Threads* reveals. Like *The Day After*, *Threads* is an attempt to portray the effect of nuclear war on a modern society. To do so, director Mick Jackson concentrates on a single medium-sized city in the heart of Great Britain: Sheffield. While he adopts a semidocumentary approach, using a narrator and titles to give information about nuclear war and filming in such a way as to mimic news footage, Jackson does develop a compelling fictional story at the heart of the film by depicting the effects of nuclear war on two families, especially on a young pregnant woman who is the only member of the families to survive the attrition of the war.

The documentary-style approach allows Jackson to communicate more or less directly to the audience, and he uses this direct communication to establish his ethical appeal. As we have already seen, the complexity of the question of nuclear arms gives a clear advantage to someone who impresses the audience as knowledgeable about the subject. Unable to master the difficult subject completely ourselves, we will be forced to place our trust in experts. Hence, as we have seen, antinuclear fiction produces a number of heroes who are scientists or members of the military establishment.

To be sure, Jackson is not, himself, a scientist or a military expert, nor does he employ such experts in key roles in his film. He does, however, communicate unequivocally his mastery of the facts of nuclear war by giving us specific statistics about it through the narration and the various titles that explain or comment on the action. He specifies, for example, the megatonnage of explosive power used in the war in general and how much of that megatonnage was dropped on Great Britain to extrapolate specific projections of the level of damage such a strike would cause. All of this specific information gives us the impression that Jackson has thoroughly researched the subject, an impression that is supported by the long list of scientific consultants in the final credits of the film.

Of course, while we are watching the film, we must have some way of judging that these facts are the result of research and not simply figures invented to make a case. The data about nuclear war that Jackson presents and the conclusions he reaches based on that data are often not self-evident, and the ordinary viewer will not have time to check them as the film progresses. If we suspect that these statistics are inaccurate, we may question the author's intelligence or honesty. One way that Jackson attempts to maintain our confidence in the accuracy of the film is by choosing a narrator who sounds reliably scholarly—has the sort of voice that we might hear narrating an historical documentary on educational television. True, the timbre of a voice does not necessarily bear any relationship to the intelligence or integrity of the speaker, but it may well inspire the audience with the all important *impression* that the speaker is knowledgeable and trustworthy.

More importantly, Jackson is careful to include verifiable facts in the script alongside the more arcane information. For example, the nuclear war develops out of a crisis between the Soviet Union and the United States involving Middle East oil fields that are crucial to the economic and political interests of both countries. Thus, Jackson has chosen a flash point that, in its importance, could conceivably bring about the sort of conflict that might spark nuclear war. Most of the potential audience would recognize these facts and would, therefore, be in a position to conclude that the director had the intelligence and political sophistication to choose one of the most likely battlefields for the first maneuvers of a cataclysmic war. At the same time, Jackson develops the crisis over a realistic length of time—more than two months—before allowing it to explode into nuclear war. In this respect, *Threads* will seem far more plausible to an audience than, for example, *The Day After,* which brings its crisis to a nuclear boil in less than a week. Our experience of international crises tells us that Jackson displays a greater attention to the pace of such crises than Meyer does in his film, and this fact, again, increases our sense of his intelligence and knowledge.

Our examination of the ethical appeal tells us that the director of *Threads* must also project a sense of his integrity and good will. Once again, the demeanor of the narrator aids him in this task. At all times, he remains calm and deliberate, never stooping to sensationalism. His description of the so-called nuclear winter exemplifies these qualities: "Hanging in the atmosphere, the clouds of debris shut out the sun's light. Across large areas of the northern hemisphere, it starts to get dark. It starts to get cold. In the centers of large land masses like America or Russia, the temperature drop may be severe, as much as twenty-five degrees centigrade. Even in Britain, within days of the attack, it could fall to freezing or below for long, dark periods." He presents his facts simply without emotional embellishment. He is even careful to qualify those facts when qualification seems to be in order. Our overriding impression of the narrator's—and, therefore, the director's—character is of someone who is forthright, accurate, and straightforward. All of these qualities, of course, help convince us of his integrity and, by projection, of the director's.

At the same time, the nature of the work implies Jackson's good will. We presume that he is making a film about the dangers of nuclear war because he cares about the survival of society. Some of this concern is evident in the opening narration: "In an urban society, everything connects. Each person's needs are filled by the skills of many others. Our lives are woven together in a fabric. But the connections that make society strong, also make it vulnerable."[2] Here Jackson's sympathy for humanity is evident in his appreciation of civilizations's vulnerability, and we can assume that this sympathy is at least one of the motivating factors of the film. The director further increases our confidence that *Threads* is motivated by actual human concern rather than by pro-Soviet bias by making the Soviets the aggressors—they invade Iran, and they fire the first tactical nuclear weapon. While blame does ultimately seem to attach to both sides in the conflict, this detail may help win the allegiance of conservative British or American viewers, who might otherwise mistrust the film's political motives.

In addition to projecting a strong sense of his own ethical appeal, however, Jackson also employs special ethical appeals through his choice of characters. To some extent, for example, he incorporates the traditional ethical appeal of legal authority into the fictional story by putting various facts and opinions about nuclear war into the mouths of the civilian leaders charged with maintaining order during and after the nuclear attack. These authorities, who are largely portrayed sympathetically, debate the hard choices that nuclear war introduces—whether or not food should be distributed to people who are unable to work, how social order can be maintained, how a growing number of homeless refugees can be sheltered—all the while expressing their rage against the events that have made such choices necessary. The ethical appeal of the youth also manifests itself in the fact that Ruth, Jimmy, and their friends are all young adults whose early deaths rebuke the concept of total war. The most powerful and important of the created ethical appeals in *Threads,* however, is that of the nurturing woman. The film's main character is Ruth Beckett, who survives the nuclear war only to face a desperate struggle for life in the postapocalyptic world. Because she is pregnant through much of the film and must fight to maintain the life of her child both before and after it is born, she powerfully evokes humanity's drive to create and nourish life even in the face of overwhelming odds.

Jackson emphasizes Ruth's role as the nourishing mother figure from the very beginning of the film. We first see her and Jimmy on a date which ends with their making love in his car. The implication that their daughter is conceived in the scene is supported by the fact that we next see them a few weeks later discussing the pregnancy. And while her initial reaction to her condition is understandably anxious, she does not seem to consider terminating it; when Jimmy's parents mention abortion, he says that neither he nor Ruth wants her to have one. Thus, her overriding urge is to nurture the life that she carries. Indeed, after Jimmy agrees to marry her, she enthusiastically indulges her domestic instincts. When he confesses his anxieties about marrying and becoming a parent, she airily dismisses his fears: "Don't be silly. It'll be lovely. I just know it will." On one level, of course, this statement is an ironic foreshadowing of the disaster that is to come. At the same time, however, it shows how eagerly Ruth embraces her maternal role.

Even the wholesale slaughter of nuclear war does not diminish Ruth's maternal instincts. True, at one point, out of panic and grief at the probable loss of her fiance, she says, "I wish I didn't have this baby," but this is a passing—and, again, humanly understandable—reaction. In the same scene she expresses anxiety at what the bomb's radiation is doing to her child, and we soon see that her concern for the baby's health supersedes her concern for her mother and father—she gulps down much of the family's milk supply, presumably in order to nourish her baby. The most obvious evidence of the triumph of Ruth's maternal instincts, however, occurs in the birth scene itself. Alone in a barn, Ruth delivers her child, and, crying with pain and joy, she rips the umbilical cord with her teeth and clutches the little girl to her breast. The elemental nature of this scene eloquently evokes the special connection between mother and child.

Jackson relies heavily on the effect of these ethical appeals in making his rational case. An enthymemic statement of the film's point is delivered by a woman protester at an antinuclear rally early in the film:

> This time they are playing with, at best, the destruction of life as we know it, and at worst, with total annihilation. You cannot win a nuclear war. Now just suppose the Russians win this war. What exactly would they be winning? What would they have conquered? Well, I'll tell you. All major centers of population and of industry would have been destroyed. . . . Oil refineries would have been destroyed. All our water would have been polluted. The soil would have been irradiated. Farm stock would be dead, diseased, or dying. The Russians would have conquered a corpse of a country.

The plausibility of this statement is founded on the conception the film conveys that the structures of modern societies are complex and, therefore, fragile and that the capacity for nuclear war to disturb those structures exceeds the immediately apparent destructive potential of the weapons used. But a further implication of the woman's speech, which may not be immediately evident, is that nuclear war threatens not only the lateral connections between various aspects of society, but also the vertical connections between present generations and future ones.

The facts Jackson offers—and the dramatic exemplification of the impact of those facts on the characters in the film—present the case that even a small nuclear exchange can destroy a society by severing the lateral connections that support it. A title tells us that the total explosive power unleashed by the war is 3,000 megatons, 210 of which fall on Great Britain. While this number may sound high, we can learn from other sources that it is about one-third the megatonnage of what would be described as a full-scale nuclear war. Schell, for example, posits a war in which 10,000 megatons are exploded in making his argument for the potential destruction of life on Earth in a nuclear war.[3] Freeman Dyson mentions the same figure in describing the stress of a full-scale nuclear war.[4] Thus, while the level of nuclear megatonnage in *Threads* is greater than that posited in the novel *Warday,* Jackson follows Strieber and Kunetka's strategy by demonstrating the effect of even a "limited" nuclear war on a modern industrial society. Because of the vulnerability of the "threads" that connect the parts of such a society, we discover that the effect would be devastating.

We are told, for example, that the direct blast, heat, and radiation effects of a 210 megaton strike on Great Britain would kill seventeen to thirty-eight million people, roughly one-fourth to one-half of the population. As horrifying as such a statistic is, it represents only the beginning of the destructiveness of a nuclear war. Ultimately more devastating to the continuance of civilization than the immediate human casualties is the disruption of the fabric of modern society. To this end the film points out the dangers of the EMP effect to electrical systems, and the consequent failure of other systems that depend on electricity—communications, plumbing, lighting, and so forth. Jackson also makes it clear that insufficient stocks of food in the short run and the effects of radiation and "nuclear winter" in the long run would lead to famine. Added to this secondary cause of death is the threat of disease plagues spread by vermin feeding on unburied corpses. Ultimately, Jackson gives us a title that makes his point: "3–8 years after attack population reaches minimum. UK numbers may decline to mediaeval levels Possibly between 4 and 11 million." This statement is followed by scenes of daily life in postapocalyptic Great Britain designed to show that the quality of life has also been reduced to medieval levels. Thus, by the end of the film, Jackson has effectively verified half of the enthymemic statement of the woman protester, that nuclear war would, indeed, destroy "life as we know it."

The second conclusion of the woman's enthymeme, that nuclear war could result in "total annihilation," is somewhat more problematical. When most people think of total annihilation in connection with nuclear war, they probably think of the human race being destroyed by the direct blast and radiation effects of the explosions themselves. The fact, then, that the direct loss of life from the war, while terrible, does not constitute the total annihilation of Great Britain, may seem to refute the woman protester's more devastating conclusion. In fact, however, the basic plot of the film exemplifies the power of nuclear war to disrupt not only the lateral connections of society but also the vertical connection: human reproduction. By citing the dangers of nuclear radiation to the reproductive system—a system in its own way as delicate as the technological network of society—Jackson calls into doubt the ultimate capacity of the human species to survive the long-term effects of nuclear war. Because he makes this case largely through the portrayal of the effects of war on a pregnant woman and her daughter, it enjoys the weight of the woman's ethical appeal.

I have already noted that many see the drive to generate and nourish life as the core of the unique ethical appeal of women. In this view, the woman's capacity to bear children comes to represent the potential for the continuity of the human race. Thus, by threatening to destroy that potential and interrupt that continuity, nuclear weapons would seem to be directly at odds with the woman's character. This concept is at the heart of Caldicott's views when she speaks of the role of women in antinuclear activism:

> The age of women has arrived. If we don't stand up and rapidly become elected to the highest offices in the country and change America's national policies from those of death to those of life, we will all be exterminated. I don't mean that in doing this women should abrogate their positive feminine principle of nurturing, loving, caring, and emotions. (Margaret Thatcher, Golda Meir, and Indira Gandhi became, in fact, men.) I mean they should tenaciously preserve these values but also learn to find and use their incredible power. The positive feminine principle must become the guiding moral principle in world politics.[5]

These sentiments seem to underpin much of *Threads*. Certainly the choice of a woman to deliver the principle thematic statement in the film fits in well with Caldicott's views—whether by design or accident. More crucially, the fact of Ruth's pregnancy—and the determination with which she brings her child to term and protects her—seems to serve as an unspoken rebuke to the carnage that nuclear war creates in the film. In this respect, a key scene occurs a week after the blast when Ruth abandons her family's basement fallout shelter to look for Jimmy. During a nightmarish walk through the still smoldering ruins, she encounters various sights ranging from the horrifying to the pitiable: charred and twisted bodies, wounded survivors waiting in vain for help, people sitting uncomprehendingly in the ruins of their homes.

Almost half of the images pertain directly to family life, especially to the link between mothers and children. Ruth sees one woman stumbling through the rubble holding a child's coat and calling the name Mandy. A little boy wanders by looking for his mother. Most vivid of all is the sight of a woman clutching the charred body of a baby to her breast. The woman stares accusingly at Ruth as she wanders by, and that sense of accusation in her look provides the visual expression of the underlying opposition between the woman's ethical appeal and nuclear war. Of course, we cannot help reflecting on Ruth's own baby in the scene, and she, herself, recalls the image later in the film when thinking about her pregnancy.

As the film reaches its climax, we see that the implied connection between Ruth and the woman in the ruins is prophetic. Ruth does manage to bring her baby to term, but the child is born retarded. While Ruth is alive, she is able to care for her daughter and protect her—to provide the nurturing that the woman's ethical appeal emphasizes. But after Ruth's premature death at about age thirty, the daughter is left to wander in a world that she does not understand. She finds herself pregnant after being raped by a boy about her own age, who also seems to be retarded. When the baby is due, the daughter, lacking Ruth's emotional resources, must beg help from an overburdened hospital worker in delivering the child. When it is placed in her arms, she recoils from the bloody sight, reacting either to some deformity in the child or to a situation that she simply cannot understand. In contrast to the cry of joy with which Ruth greeted her baby's birth, the film ends with the daughter's look of anguished confusion and fear.

The retardation of the daughter and her apparent rejection of her own child suggest a deterioration of the line of human continuity. Radiation from the bombs has attacked the most delicate thread that ties civilization together: the link between one generation and the next. Although the example we see here is too limited for us to conclude that *Threads* actually is portraying the beginning of the end for the human race, it is sufficient to raise the specter of the destruction of the species and make us confront the possibility.

We can see, then, that the clearest enthymemic statements of Jackson's case are delivered by voices that embody the two strongest ethical appeals developed in the film. The danger of nuclear war is set out by the woman protester, and her importance as a representative of a specifically woman's appeal is emphasized by the fact that the chief focus of that appeal, Ruth, is seen repeatedly in the crowd listening to the woman's words. The explication of how nuclear war could achieve the level of destruction that the woman implies is given by the voice of the narrator in his prologue about the vulnerability of society. The extent to which the authors have succeeded in creating strong ethical appeals here, then, may influence the audience's tendency to accept these enthymemic arguments.

At the same time that the use of rational appeal in *Threads* depends on the ethical appeal for its full effect, it also helps to arouse the emotional appeal. On the most basic level, the images that the film uses to exemplify the facts it is communicating will arouse an immediate emotional reaction in us. It is difficult to remain emotionless while experiencing images of people being hit with flying shards of glass, a child buried under a pile of rubble, or a woman holding the charred body of her baby. And, as the characters whose experiences illustrate the rational case against nuclear war become more familiar to us, our emotional reactions will increase. We are told that two-thirds of the houses in Britain are in possible fire zones and then shown Jimmy's parents trying to beat back a fire in their home. Rather than simply informing us of the symptoms of radiation sickness, Jackson shows us graphic scenes of Ruth's family vomiting. To illustrate the fact that there are ten to twenty million unburied corpses in Great Britain, he gives us an image of dogs and rats gnawing on the body of Ruth's grandmother. To make the concept of postwar famine vivid, he treats us to the sight of Ruth putting four dead rats into her grocery bag.

Much of the same point can be made about Jackson's use of situation and plot in the film. We have already seen that the basic situation in the film, and the plot that grows out of it—Ruth's pregnancy at the time of a nuclear war and her efforts to maintain her own and her daughter's life through that war—develop Jackson's rational case. At the same time the sight of Ruth, pregnant and alone, struggling to bring her pregnancy to term in the postwar wasteland inherently begs our pity. And the joy we might share with her when the baby is born is tempered by our realization that the child probably has been damaged in some way by the effects of radiation. Moreover, the image of Ruth's daughter recoiling in fear and revulsion when *her* baby is born is bound to provoke our pity and dread as well.

On one level, the dynamic of our emotional reactions to plot and situation parallel that of our emotional reactions to the images: we respond directly to what we see on the screen, and our knowledge that what we see is the result of nuclear war should mobilize our emotions against nuclear weapons. As we have seen in an earlier chapter, however, our realization of the theme of the piece can also provoke an emotional reaction. It is frightening to witness a representation of the destructiveness of nuclear war, but it may be even more frightening to know that even a small war could exploit society's vulnerability to the extent that civilization would collapse. It is, of course, more terrifying still to reflect that the effects of radiation on the equally vulnerable human reproductive system could spell the beginning of the end of the human race as we know it. Thus, the film arouses our emotions not only with the evidence that supports its rational points, but with the rational points themselves.

We can see, then, that *Threads* employs the ethical appeal of the authoritative source and that of the nurturing woman to present the argument that even a limited nuclear war would reduce the quality of human life severely if not destroy humanity completely. In making these points and in supporting and illustrating them, Jackson arouses the emotions of pity and fear that may increase our acceptance of the point and mobilize our energies to oppose nuclear weapons. In doing so, the director uses the three appeals to support and influence each other.

Threads could be used to illustrate one further aspect of anti-nuclear fiction: the mutual value of the artistic and the rhetorical aspects of a persuasive fiction. Any artistic effort involves choice. An author will place characters with certain selected characteristics into selected situations to perform selected actions. The motives that influence his choices can be varied: emotional, biographical, historical, psychological, and so forth. Those motives can also be rhetorical. The author's desire to make some particular point—whether that point is social, political, philosophical, or moral—may influence his choice of character, situation, plot, and imagery, and that influence can be as valid and as effective as another author's desire to explore his own psyche or chronicle his exploration of the human condition.

Without claiming any special insight into Jackson's mind, I think we can speculate about how the rhetorical nature of the work might have interacted with its artistic aspects. The director's desire to suggest the ultimate capacity of nuclear war to destroy the human race may have influenced his selection of Ruth, a pregnant woman, as the main character. It also, no doubt, urged the basic movement of the plot, since the need to deal with the long-range effects of the war on the gene pool demanded not only that Ruth's daughter be born alive but that she be able to bear her own child. Fortunately, the time span that such a plot requires fits in well with Jackson's parallel desire to demonstrate how devastating a nuclear war would be to the fabric of society. Even after the thirteen years required for Ruth's daughter to grow to puberty, the connections between the segments of society have not been repaired sufficiently to return civilization to its prewar level.

On a more particular level, the facts of nuclear warfare dictate much of the imagery in the film. Jackson must find visual methods of depicting the various destructive forces of nuclear weapons: the EMP effect, the heat wave, the radiation from the blast and fallout, nuclear winter, dramatic increases in ultraviolet radiation, and so forth. And so we see power lines and telephone wires shorting out under the strain from the electromagnetic pulse. We see the face of Jimmy's mother horribly burned from the heat wave. We see people in the throes of radiation sickness vomiting bloody tissue. We see people starving while the able-bodied struggle to harvest shriveled crops. We see people wearing hoods and goggles to protect themselves from the cancer and cataracts that ultraviolet radiation causes. By the end of the film we see people grown old before their time in a fragile, primitive society. All of these images are mandated by Jackson's need to depict essential aspects of nuclear war. At the same time, the need to explain these various facets of the war urges the use of narration and titles that clarify the action and, therefore, increase our understanding of the characters and the dramatic conflicts they face.

By the same token, many of the artistic choices, by reinforcing and illustrating the message, make it more persuasive. In presenting us with a fairly limited set of characters with whom to identify, Jackson helps to focus our perceptions of the horrors of nuclear war. And the details we are given about these characters' lives—their occupations, their hobbies, their hopes, and their fears—insure that we will know them well enough to feel their pain intensely when the suffering comes. I have already mentioned how one of the fictional elements—the plot—serves to reveal one part of the film's message, but we can also detect Jackson's efforts to communicate that message more subtly. The motif suggested in the title is a major example. It is introduced at the beginning of the film with the image of a spider spinning a thread of webbing while the narrator explains that society is so vulnerable because of the delicate links between its parts. Obviously the spider web is a metaphor for society, and the filaments of the web—the *Threads* of the title—are the connections that make society both strong and vulnerable. After this opening, Jackson uses images of threads—or analogous filaments—throughout the film. During the attack itself, we see electrical wires destroyed by the EMP effect. When Ruth delivers her daughter, she must chew the umbilical cord in two, an action that depicts the primitive level of her society as well as symbolizing the severing of the genetic connections between generations. Near the end of the film, we see Ruth's daughter and some other children removing threads from a piece of cloth, apparently in an effort to salvage them for use in a garment. The action exemplifies and symbolizes the efforts of the society as a whole to salvage what threads remain of the "garment" that was civilization in order to fashion a new, if more primitive world.

We can see, then, that the rhetorical and the artistic elements in *Threads* are not necessarily inimical to each other. In fact, Jackson is able to use the rhetorical elements to inform and guide his artistic vision, and the artistic elements to embody and give force to his rhetorical message. In the final analysis, the two aspects of the work live or die together. Only if the film succeeds artistically—only if it moves the viewer—will it have a chance to succeed rhetorically. At the same time, the viewer who is determined to resist the rhetorical message will probably resist the aesthetic experience of the film as well. In this respect, Jackson shares the burdens of all writers of rhetorical fiction. By creating a work in which rhetoric and art are both so crucial to the ultimate effect, he has multiplied the ways in which he can fail. The fact that *Threads* succeeds—and succeeds so well—is a tribute to his and his collaborators' skills as both artists and rhetoricians. It is also a tribute to the potential power of art and rhetoric to nourish and reinforce each other.

9

The Effect of Antinuclear Fiction

In the last chapter of *Weapons and Hope*, Freeman Dyson muses about the place of literature in mankind's effort to find meaning in the nuclear world: "Through the writings of the war poets we share the agonies of the two world wars. Literature ties us together. Through literature we know our roots. Through literature we become friends and colleagues of our predecessors. Through literature they talk to us of their troubles and confusions and give us courage to deal with our own."[1] While Dyson is speaking here specifically about how one generation finds insight about timeless issues from the writings of its ancestors, he might just as well be speaking of how members of a single generation can speak to each other about particular issues of its day, including the most vital issue of our day: nuclear weapons. Dyson speaks of the power of literature to infuse its readers with a sense of meaning and purpose. And certainly we have seen enough examples of antinuclear literature that attempt to do both.

True, antinuclear fiction often paints a dark picture of humanity and its future, but it does so only to arouse that sense of meaning and purpose that the nuclear age threatens to numb. It terrifies us out of our complacency with its vision of destruction, but it also strengthens our resolve by maintaining either implicitly or explicitly that that dark prediction need not come true. Occasionally, it even offers us specific strategies for avoiding armageddon.

And we can assume that it will continue to do so for the foreseeable future. True, at the time of this writing in late 1990, the apparent breakdown of the Soviet system seems about to change the international situation permanently. But, as I have already suggested, these changes do not necessarily guarantee relief from the nuclear dilemma. Quite simply, as long as nuclear weapons exist, the danger of their use exists, and any use of these weapons carries with it the awesome potential of global disaster that has always been the trump card of antinuclear fiction.

We cannot predict what course the world will take in relation to nuclear weapons. Volatile changes carry with them dangerous potentialities, and the breakdown of "the evil empire" may leave the Soviet arsenal in hands less controlled than those which have been poised over the nuclear buttons for the last forty-five years. If so, the dangers of nuclear catastrophe in the future may well dwarf the nightmare through which we have lived the past half century.

But even if the movements of the early 1990s *do* mark the beginnings of permanent peace and cooperation between East and West, the potential for small scale nuclear war still exists. At the beginning of the nuclear age, when the United States controlled the bomb, this country used the threat of its use to solve international conflicts. Certain reactions in the wake of the Iraqi invasion of Kuwait in 1990 suggest that such a dynamic could easily reassert itself in the absence of a threat of all out war with the Soviet Union.

Indeed, the possibility of limited use of the weapons rises as the possibility of global nuclear war recedes. The specter of an ongoing series of Hiroshima and Nagasaki bombings designed to solve the sorts of minor conflicts that have peppered the international scene during the last forty-five years, while obviously less threatening than global nuclear war, is still terrible to contemplate. And—as World War I showed—even small conflicts can become unpredictably large in a volatile international climate.

Even assuming that the great powers have learned their lesson about the dangers of the nuclear arsenal, widespread nuclear proliferation during the last forty-five years has left these weapons in the hands of nations and leaders who may see them as a necessary bulwark against overwhelming antagonistic forces. Israel, for example, is widely believed to have nuclear weapons. It takes little imagination to foresee the Israelis' using such weapons if they believed their country was about to be overrun.

As I have already pointed out, there is always a possibility that nuclear weapons will fall into hands of third world forces that are predictable only in their hostility to the West in general and the United States in particular. The fact that Iraq was attempting to develop nuclear weapons was one factor involved in the Persian Gulf crisis of 1990–1991. And the fear that terrorists might begin to arm themselves with even primitive atomic bombs is a very real one.

So while the human race has turned some kind of corner in its relationship with its most deadly invention, it is far from having solved the dilemma that that invention presents. The future offers the promise of new hope for an end to that dilemma, but it also poses new challenges. Our future thinking about nuclear weapons will have to reflect those new hopes and attempt to answer those new challenges.

And, as it has in the past, antinuclear fiction will reflect our methods of dealing with the changed nature of the nuclear threat. We have already seen how the HBO film *By Dawn's Early Light* has responded to the shift in the nuclear climate by demonstrating how nuclear war could occur in an age of *glasnost*. The future may hold novels and films that detail the dangers of nuclear intimidation by the major powers, third-world threats of nuclear war, terrorist uses of nuclear weapons, or other dangers we cannot yet imagine.

But, we might ask, to what end? Just how effective is antinuclear fiction at achieving its goals? Have the various works we have been examining here succeeded in galvanizing public opinion against nuclear weapons? Is the world a safer place because of the efforts of the artists we have been discussing?

The answer, unfortunately, is problematical. It is difficult enough to gauge internal movements of the human will, let alone to determine how much any given stimulus has contributed to that movement. Too often our statements about the effect of individual efforts at persuasion will have to remain as disappointingly impressionistic as Stephen Farber's remarks about Kramer's adaptation of Shute's novel: "*On the Beach* was acclaimed in Moscow as well as New York, and some observers believed that it influenced the United States and the Soviet Union's decision to ban aboveground nuclear tests."[2] Obviously, such a statement is too vague and unsubstantiated to convince us of the effectiveness of antinuclear fiction. Even if we point to evidence like Helen Caldicott's statement that the genesis of her opposition to nuclear weapons was her reading of Shute's novel,[3] such individual testimony says nothing about the potential of fiction to persuade a mass audience.

The era of the national opinion poll does give us access to the accumulated individual testimonies of mass audiences. But, if we are to judge the effect of a single work on such an audience, we would have to arrange for the members of that audience to experience the work more or less simultaneously so that we could be sure that extraneous factors had not entered into whatever shifts of opinion we might record. The single instance of such a nationwide phenomenon in relation to the nuclear-weapons issue is, of course, the national broadcast of the ABC television film *The Day After* in November 1983. Unfortunately, the results of a Warner-Amex Qube cable network poll reported in the *New York Times* two days after the broadcast found no dramatic shift one way or the other in the opinions of those who viewed the film.[4] Of those who had watched *The Day After,* only 12 percent had shifted to a support of arms control, and only 6 percent reported that they had adopted a stronger defense stance. A later study conducted by George Washington University on 928 people reinforced the perception that the film had had negligible impact on the political views of the people who viewed it.[5] Before seeing the film, 78 percent of those studied by George Washington favored a nuclear freeze and 13 percent opposed such a move. These percentages remained virtually the same after the study group had viewed the film.

We may be making a mistake, however, in judging the worth of persuasive fiction in general on the ability of any one work to cause significant shifts in mass opinion. It would not be surprising if, in matters of important policy, people made up their minds slowly and deliberately. Significant shifts in attitude among the public at large may, depending on the issue involved, take a generation or more to manifest themselves. Given this state of affairs, it would be unreasonable to expect that any one work could change public attitudes about nuclear weapons to any measurable degree.

Instead, we might better speculate about the cumulative effect on public opinion of the body of antinuclear work we have been studying. We might more profitably ask if the presence of these various works in the national culture has contributed to some change in overall attitudes toward nuclear weapons during the last forty years. And, indeed, there is some evidence to suggest that American opinion in general has shifted increasingly in an antinuclear direction during that time period. In November 1983, *Newsweek* cited two polls on public attitudes toward nuclear weapons. The first, a Gallup poll taken in 1946, revealed that 73 percent of Americans favored the continued development of nuclear weapons. A 1983 Roper poll indicated that 67 percent of Americans favored a bilateral freeze on such development.[6]

Of course, any number of factors may have contributed to this shift. Certainly the fact that the Soviet Union developed its own atomic bomb in 1949 might have caused at least part of the American public to reconsider its position. The development of the hydrogen bomb and of more rapid and more accurate delivery systems no doubt also increased the public's perception of the danger of nuclear weapons.

At the same time, it is also likely that an ongoing stream of antinuclear messages has contributed to the general rejection of nuclear arms. *Newsweek* cited another Roper poll that examined public anxiety about nuclear weapons in 1974 and in 1983 and found that the number of people who feared that nuclear war would become a serious problem in the next half century increased from 47 percent to 71 percent.[7] Significantly, this dramatic rise in concern about nuclear weapons occurred during a decade in which no dramatic breakthroughs in nuclear technology occurred to pique public fears. Moreover, the Warner-Amex Qube poll cited above indicated that the single significant difference in the attitudes of people before and after watching *The Day After* was that afterward more people were concerned about the imminence of nuclear war: after watching the film, 88 percent of those polled said that they regarded nuclear war as a real threat and worried about it to a significant degree as opposed to 26 percent who said they did so before viewing the film. True, this newfound concern was probably fleeting for many or most of those polled, but the phenomenon does point up the ability of fiction to arouse such concerns. We can only speculate about how the more or less constant stream of antinuclear works over a forty year period has helped to erode the complacency of the American public about nuclear weapons.

It is not unreasonable, then to suggest that at least part of the shift in American attitudes toward nuclear weapons may well have been influenced by antinuclear fiction. Once again, however, I would not maintain that significant changes result from the public's experience of any single work of antinuclear fiction, but rather from a general pattern of such experiences. Little by little such a pattern, by repeating and reinforcing the arguments against nuclear weapons, infiltrates the consciousness of a nation. Little by little people begin to accept attitudes that are inimical to the presence of such weapons. In the last forty-five years, the American consciousness has undergone such a change, and we can be confident, if not empirically certain, that antinuclear fiction has helped to bring about that change.

At least in part as a result of antinuclear fiction, then, the American public has grown less naive about the potential consequences of nuclear weapons. We are no longer as inclined to see them as the convenient big stick with which we can walk softly through the world. We can now see their existence as a tragedy waiting to occur—a deadly dilemma that must finally be resolved.

The nature of that final resolution is ultimately up to us. Only we can decide whether we will lay down our weapons or destroy ourselves with them. This fact is the underlying source of both the horror and the hope of Miller's *Canticle for Leibowitz* and Hoban's *Riddley Walker*. For each of these novelists, the best—the only— hope for mankind's future lies in fundamental choices of the human heart.

It is, of course, to that same human heart that fiction addresses itself. Such being the case, antinuclear fiction may offer a uniquely effective method for teaching the vital lessons of this hazardous age. Hoban makes this point at the end of *Riddley Walker* when he sends his hero out into the world to preach the antinuclear message through the medium of a Punch and Judy show. And, ultimately, if modern man is like X-127—imprisoned in the nightmare of the nuclear age—he is also like Riddley—possessed of the power to escape that nightmare. Like Riddley, the people of the world can discover in fiction the horror of their technology of destruction and the hope—and the sense of moral purpose—that will help them overcome that technology.

Notes

Preface

1. William M. Arkin and Richard W. Fieldhouse, *Nuclear Battlefields: Global Links in the Nuclear Arms Race* (Cambridge, Mass.: Ballinger, 1985), 38.
2. Ibid.

Chapter 1. Rhetoric and Fiction

1. O. G. Brockett, "Poetry as Instrument," in *Papers in Rhetoric and Poetic,* ed. Donald C. Bryant (Iowa City: University of Iowa Press, 1965), 17.
2. Horace, *The Art of Poetry,* in *Plato to Alexander Pope,* ed. Walter and Vivian Sutton (N.Y.: Odyssey Press, 1966), 80–81.
3. Sir Philip Sidney, "The Defense of Poesy," in *Plato to Alexander Pope,* ed. Walter and Vivian Sutton (N.Y.: Odyssey Press, 1966), 127.
4. Ibid., 129.
5. M. H. Abrams, *The Mirror and the Lamp* (London: Oxford University Press, 1953), 22.
6. William Wordsworth, "Preface to the Second Edition of *The Lyrical Ballads,*" in *English Romance Writers,* ed. David Perkins (N.Y.: Harcourt, Brace & World, Inc., 1967), 322.
7. Percy Bysshe Shelley, "A Defense of Poetry," in *English Romantic Writers,* ed. David Perkins (N.Y.: Harcourt, Brace & World, Inc., 1967), 1087.
8. James L. Kinneavy, *A Theory of Discourse* (N.Y.: W. W. Norton & Co., 1980), 329.
9. Raman Selden, *A Reader's Guide to Contemporary Literary Theory 2nd ed.* (Lexington: University of Kentucky Press, 1989), 65.
10. Stanley Fish, *Is There a Text in This Class?* (Cambridge, Mass.: Harvard University Press, 1980), 27.
11. Terry Eagleton, *Literary Theory: An Introduction* (Minneapolis: University of Minnesota Press, 1984), 147.
12. A. P. Foulkes, *Literature and Propaganda* (N.Y.: Methuen, 1983), 30.
13. Marshall Davidson, *The Writer's America* (N.Y.: American Heritage Publishing Co., Inc., 1973), 184.

Chapter 2. The Dynamic of the Ethical Appeal in Fiction

1. Aristotle, *Rhetoric,* ed. Lane Cooper (Englewood Cliffs, N.J.: Prentice Hall, Inc., 1932), 9 (Bk. I, ch. 2).
2. Ibid., 92 (Bk. II, ch. 1).

3. Bertrand Russell, *Has Man a Future?* (London: George Allen & Unwin, Ltd., 1961), 73.
4. Ibid., 72.
5. Freeman Dyson, *Weapons and Hope* (N.Y.: Harper & Row, 1984), 92.
6. Ibid., 93.
7. Ephraim Katz, *The Film Encyclopedia* (N.Y.: Perigree, 1982), 903.
8. All quotations from this novel are from Philip Wylie, *Triumph* (N.Y.: Doubleday & Co., Inc., 1963).
9. All quotations from this novel are from Mordecai Roshwald, *Level 7* (N.Y.: Signet).

Chapter 3. The Cast of Characters

1. Peter Wyden, *Day One* (N.Y.: Warner Books, 1985), 175–76.
2. Edward Zuckerman, *The Day after World War III* (N.Y.: Viking, 1984), 76.
3. Ibid., 80–81.
4. Helen Caldicott, *Missile Envy* (N.Y.: Bantam, 1985), 362.
5. All quotations from this novel are from C. P. Snow, *The New Men* (London: Macmillan, 1954).
6. Zuckerman, *The Day after World War III*, 43.
7. All quotations from this novel are from Eugene Burdick and Harvey Wheeler, *Fail-Safe* (N.Y.: Dell, 1962).
8. Zuckerman, *The Day after World War III*, 71.
9. Ernest Lefever and E. Stephen Hunt, eds., *The Apocalyptic Premise* (Washington, D.C.: Ethics and Public Policy Center, 1982), 339–49.
10. Lefever and Hunt, *The Apocalyptic Premise*, 297–98.
11. Jerry Falwell, *Listen, America* (N.Y.: Doubleday, 1980), 98.
12. All quotations from this novel are from Walter M. Miller, Jr. *A Canticle for Leibowitz* (N.Y.: Bantam, 1982).
13. All quotations from this source are from Whitley Strieber and James Kunetka, *Warday* (N.Y.: Holt, Rinehart and Winston, 1984).
14. All quotations from this film are from *Testament*, Lynne Littman, dir., Paramount, 1983.
15. Caldicott, *Missile Envy*, 334.
16. All quotations from this film are from *Wargames*, John Badham, dir., United Artists, 1983.

Chapter 4. The Rational Appeal in Fiction

1. Larry Arnhart, *Aristotle on Political Reasoning* (DeKalb, Ill.: Northern Illinois University Press, 1986), 6.
2. Ibid., 7.
3. Ibid., 40–41.
4. George F. Kennan, *The Nuclear Delusion* (N.Y.: Random House, 1983), 127–33.
5. Aristotle, *Rhetoric*, 155–56 (Bk. II, ch. 22).
6. Zuckerman, *The Day after World War III*, 73–74.
7. Arnhart, *Aristotle on Political Reasoning*, 47.
8. Zuckerman, *The Day after World War III*, 60–61n.

9. Dore Schary, *The Highest Tree* (N.Y.: Random House, 1960), 114.

10. William Bayer, *The Great Movies* (N.Y.: Grossett & Dunlap, 1973), 80.

11. All quotations from this film are from *Dr. Strangelove: or: How I Learned to Stop Worrying and Love the Bomb*, Stanley Kubrick, dir., Columbia, 1964.

12. Zuckerman, *The Day after World War III*, 64.

13. Aristotle, *Rhetoric*, 149 (Bk. II, ch. 20).

14. Dyson, *Weapons and Hope*, 33–34.

15. Paul R. Ehrlich, et al., *The Cold and the Dark* (N.Y.: W. W. Norton, 1984), xiii–xiv.

16. Sharon Begley and John Barry, "A Milder Nuclear Winter," *Newsweek* 31 March 1986, 65.

17. Joseph Fromm, "The Day after *The Day After,*" *U.S. News and World Report* 5 December 1983, 29.

18. All quotations from this novel are from Russell Hoban, *Riddley Walker* (N.Y.: Simon and Schuster, 1982).

Chapter 5. The Nuclear Debate in Fiction

1. Wyden, *Day One*, 132.

2. Ibid., 166–67.

3. Zuckerman, *The Day after World War III*, 39.

4. Ibid., 71.

5. Wyden, *Day One*, 317.

6. Pearl S. Buck, *Command the Morning* (N.Y.: Pocket Books, 1967), 232.

7. All quotations from this novel are from Aldous Huxley, *Ape and Essence* (N.Y.: Harper and Row, 1948).

8. Zuckerman, *The Day after World War III*, 72.

9. *The Day the Earth Stood Still*, Robert Wise, dir. 20th Century-Fox Film Corporation, 1951.

10. Dyson, *Weapons and Hope*, 170–71.

11. Wyden, *Day One*, 226.

12. Zuckerman, *The Day after World War III*, 43.

13. Ibid., 187.

14. Ibid., 82.

15. Ibid.

16. Ibid., 194–95.

17. Ibid., 192.

18. Herman Kahn, *On Thermonuclear War* (Princeton: Princeton University Press, 1960), 145.

19. Caldicott, *Missile Envy*, 29.

20. Arkin and Fieldhouse, *Nuclear Battlefields*, 82.

21. Zuckerman, *The Day after World War III*, 161.

22. Arkin and Fieldhouse, *Nuclear Battlefields*, 56–59.

23. Caldicott, *Missile Envy*, 41–42.

24. William Manchester, *The Glory and the Dream* (N.Y.: Bantam, 1975), 1028.

25. Caldicott, *Missile Envy*, 178.

26. Dyson, *Weapons and Hope*, 229–31.

27. Ibid., 251.

28. Zuckerman, *The Day after World War III*, 4.

29. Ibid., 13.

30. Paul Duke, ed., *Beyond Reagan* (N.Y.: Warner Books, 1986), 196.
31. Union of Concerned Scientists, *The Fallacy of Star Wars* (N.Y.: Vintage, 1984), 149.
32. *By Dawn's Early Light*, Jack Sholder, dir., HBO Pictures, 1990.

Chapter 6. The Dynamic of the Emotional Appeal in Fiction

1. Colin Radford, "Charlton's Feelings about the Fictitious: A Reply," *British Journal of Aesthetics* 25 (1985), 383.
2. Samuel Taylor Coleridge, *Biographia Literaria,* James Engell and W. Jackson Bates eds. (Princeton, N.J.: Princeton University Press, 1983), Vol. II, 6.
3. Eva Schaper, "Fiction and the Suspension of Disbelief," *British Journal of Aesthetics,* 18 (1978), 31–44.
4. B. J. Rosebury, "Fiction, Emotion, and 'Belief': A Reply to Eva Schaper," *British Journal of Aesthetics* 19 (1979), 120–30.
5. Ibid., 122–23.
6. Jerry L. Guthrie, "Self-Deception and Emotional Response to Fiction," *British Journal of Aesthetics* 21 (1981), 65–75.
7. Kendall L. Walton, "How Remote Are Fictional Worlds from the Real World?" *Journal of Aesthetics and Art Criticism* 37 (1978), 21.
8. Peter Lamarque, "How Can We Fear and Pity Fictions?" *British Journal of Aesthetics* 21 (1981), 302.
9. William Charlton, "Feeling for the Fictitious," *British Journal of Aesthetics* 24 (1984), 206–16.
10. Barrie Paskins, "On Being Moved by Anna Karenina and *Anna Karenina,"* *Philosophy* 52 (1977), 344–47.
11. Mark Packer, "The Conditions of Aesthetic Feeling in Aristotle's Poetics," *British Journal of Aesthetics* 24 (1984), 138–47.
12. Harold Skulsky, "On Being Moved by Fiction," *Journal of Aesthetics and Art Criticism* 39 (1980), 5–14.
13. John Nolt, "Expression and Emotion," *British Journal of Aesthetics* 21 (1981), 139–50.
14. H. O. Mounce, "Art and Real Life," *Philosophy* 55 (1980), 183–92.
15. R. T. Allen, "The Reality of Responses to Fiction," *British Journal of Aesthetics* 26 (1986), 68.
16. Mounce, "Art and Real Life," 191–92.
17. John Hersey, *Hiroshima* (N.Y.: Bantam, 1975), 67.
18. Nolt, "Expression and Emotion," 149.
19. Packer, "The Conditions of Aesthetic Feelings," 144.

Chapter 7. The Emotions of Antinuclear Fiction

1. Aristotle, *Rhetoric,* 120 (Bk. II, ch. 8).
2. Aristotle, *Rhetoric,* 107 (Bk. II, ch. 5).
3. Aristotle, *Rhetoric,* 109 (Bk. II, ch. 5).
4. Robert Brustein, "Reflections on Horror Movies" in *The Third Theater* (London: Jonathan Cape, Ltd. 1970), 219.
5. Marcel Ophuls, "After the Day After," *American Film,* vol. 10 (1984), no. 2, 36.

6. Bayer, *The Great Movies*, 80.
7. Caldicott, *Missile Envy*, 319.

Chapter 8. *Threads:* A Synthesis

1. Aristotle, *Rhetoric*, 91 (Bk. II, ch. 1).
2. All quotations from this film are from *Threads*, Mick Jackson, dir., BBC-TV, 1984.
3. Jonathan Schell, *The Fate of the Earth* (N.Y.: Avon Books, 1982), 54.
4. Dyson, *Weapons and Hope*, 23.
5. Caldicott, *Missile Envy*, 322.

Chapter 9. The Effect of Antinuclear Fiction

1. Dyson, *Weapons and Hope*, 299.
2. Stephen Farber, "The End of the World, Take 1," *American Film*, vol. 8 (1982), no. 9, 62.
3. Caldicott, *Missile Envy*, 1.
4. Robert D. McFadden, "Atomic War Film Spurs Nationwide Discussion," *New York Times* 22 November 1983: A27.
5. Glenn Collins, " 'Day After' Fades but Debate on Effects Lingers," *New York Times* 19 June 1984: A12.
6. Harry F. Waters, et al., "TV's Nuclear Nightmare," *Newsweek* 21 November 1983, 72.
7. Ibid.

Bibliography

Abrams, M. H. *The Mirror and the Lamp.* London: Oxford University Press, 1953.

Allen, R. T. "The Reality of Responses to Fiction." *British Journal of Aesthetics* 26 (1986) 64–68.

Aristotle. *Rhetoric.* Edited by Lane Cooper. Reprint. Englewood Cliffs, N.J.: Prentice-Hall, Inc., 1932.

Arkin, William M., and Richard W. Fieldhouse. *Nuclear Battlefields: Global Links in the Arms Race.* Cambridge, Mass.: Ballinger, 1985.

Arnhart, Larry. *Aristotle on Political Reasoning.* DeKalb, Ill.: Northern Illinois University Press, 1986.

Bayer, William. *The Great Movies.* New York: Grosset & Dunlap, 1973.

Begley, Sharon, and John Barry. "A Milder Nuclear Winter." *Newsweek* 31 March 1986: 65.

Brockett, O. G. "Poetry as Instrument." *Papers in Rhetoric and Poetic.* Donald C. Bryant, ed. Iowa City: University of Iowa Press, 1965.

Brustein, Robert. "Reflections on Horror Movies." *The Third Theatre.* London: Jonathan Cape, Ltd., 1970. Pp. 218–30.

Buck, Pearl S. *Command the Morning.* 1959. Reprint. N.Y.: Pocket Books, 1967.

Burdick, Eugene, and Harvey Wheeler. *Fail-Safe.* 1962. Reprint. N.Y.: Dell, 1982.

By Dawn's Early Light. Dir. Jack Sholder. HBO Pictures, 1990.

Caldicott, Helen. *Missile Envy.* 1984. Reprint. N.Y.: Bantam, 1985.

Charlton, William. "Feeling for the Fictitious." *British Journal of Aesthetics* 24 (1984), 206–16.

Coleridge, Samuel Taylor. *Biographia Literaria.* James Engell and W. Jackson Bate, eds. Princeton, N.J.: Princeton University Press, 1983.

Collins, Glenn. " 'Day After' Fades, but Debate on Effects Lingers." *New York Times* 19 June 1984: A12.

Davidson, Marshall. *The Writer's America.* N.Y.: American Heritage Publishing Co., Inc., 1973.

The Day After. Dir. Nicholas Meyer. ABC Films, 1983.

The Day the Earth Stood Still. Dir. Robert Wise. 20th Century-Fox, 1951.

Dr. Strangelove or: How I Learned to Stop Worrying and Love the Bomb. Dir. Stanley Kubrick. Columbia, 1964.

Duke, Paul, ed. *Beyond Reagan.* N.Y.: Warner Books, 1986.

Dyson, Freeman. *Weapons and Hope.* N.Y.: Harper & Row, 1984.

Eagleton, Terry. *Literary Theory: An Introduction.* Minneapolis: University of Minnesota Press, 1984.

Ehrlich, Paul R., et al. *The Cold and the Dark.* N.Y.: W. W. Norton, 1985.

Falwell, Jerry. *Listen, America!* N.Y.: Doubleday, 1980.

Farber, Stephen. "The End of the World, Take 1." *American Film* October 1982: 61–63.

Fish, Stanley. *Is There a Text in This Class?* Cambridge, Mass.: Harvard University Press, 1980.

Foulkes, A. P. *Literature and Propaganda.* N.Y.: Methuen, 1983.

Fromm, Joseph, James M. Hildreth, and Orr Kelly. "The Day after the Day After." *U.S. News and World Report* 5 December 1983: 29–30.

Guthrie, Jerry L. "Self-Deception and Emotional Response to Fiction." *British Journal of Aesthetics* 21 (1981), 65–75.

Hersey, John. *Hiroshima.* 1946. N.Y.: Bantam, 1975.

Hoban, Russell. *Riddley Walker.* 1980. New York: Simon & Schuster, 1982.

Horace. *The Art of Poetry.* In *Plato to Alexander Pope.* Edited by Walter and Vivian Sutton, 72–84. N.Y.: Odyssey Press, 1966.

Huxley, Aldous. *Ape and Essence.* N.Y.: Harper and Row, 1948.

Incredible Shrinking Man. Dir. Jack Arnold. Universal, 1957.

Kahn, Herman. *On Thermonuclear War.* Princeton, N.J.: Princeton University Press, 1960.

Katz, Ephraim. *The Film Encyclopedia.* 1979. N.Y.: Perigee, 1982.

Kennan, George F. *The Nuclear Delusion.* 1982. Reprint. N.Y.: Random House, 1983.

Kinneavy, James L. *A Theory of Discourse.* N.Y.: W. W. Norton & Co., 1980.

Lamarque, Peter. "How Can We Fear and Pity Fictions?" *British Journal of Aesthetics* 21 (1981), 291–304.

Lefever, Ernest W., and E. Stephen Hunt, eds. *The Apocalyptic Premise.* Washington, D.C.: Ethics and Public Policy Center, 1982.

McFadden, Robert D. "Atomic War Film Spurs Nationwide Discussion." *New York Times* 22 November 1983: A27.

Manchester, William. *The Glory and the Dream.* 1974. Reprint. N.Y.: Bantam, 1975.

Miller, Walter M., Jr. *A Canticle for Leibowitz.* 1959. Reprint. N.Y.: Bantam, 1982.

Mounce, H. O. "Art and Real Life." *Philosophy* 55 (1980), 183–92.

Nolt, John. "Expression and Emotion," *British Journal of Aesthetics* 21 (1981), 139–50.

On the Beach. Dir. Stanley Kramer. United Artists, 1959.

Ophuls, Marcel. "After *The Day After.*" *American Film* 10.2 (1984): 33–38.

Packer, Mark. "The Conditions of Aesthetic Feeling in Aristotle's Poetics." *British Journal of Aesthetics* 24 (1984), 138–47.

Paskins, Barrie. "On Being Moved by Anna Karenina and *Anna Karenina.*" *Philosophy* 52 (1977), 344–47.

Radford, Colin. "Charlton's Feelings about the Fictitious: A Reply." *British Journal of Aesthetics* 25 (1985) 380–83.

Rosebury, B. J. "Fiction, Emotion, and 'Belief': A Reply to Eva Schaper." *British Journal of Aesthetics* 19 (1979), 120–30.

Roshwald, Mordecai. *Level 7.* 1959. Reprint. N.Y.: Signet, n.d.

Russell, Bertrand. *Has Man a Future?* London: George Allen & Unwin, Ltd., 1961.

Schaper, Eva. "Fiction and the Suspension of Disbelief." *British Journal of Aesthetics,* 18 (1978), 31–44.

Schary, Dore. *The Highest Tree.* N.Y.: Random House, 1960.

Schell, Jonathan. *The Fate of the Earth.* 1982. N.Y.: Avon Books, 1982.

Selden, Raman. *A Reader's Guide to Contemporary Literary Theory 2nd ed.* Lexington: University of Kentucky Press, 1989.

Shelley, Percy Bysshe. "A Defense of Poetry." In *English Romantic Writers,* edited by David Perkins, 1072–1087. N.Y.: Harcourt, Brace & World, Inc., 1967.

Shute, Nevil. *On the Beach.* 1957. N.Y.: Ballantine Books, 1974.

Sidney, Sir Philip. "The Defense of Poesy." In *Plato to Alexander Pope,* edited by Walter and Vivian Sutton, 121–152. N.Y.: The Odyssey Press, Inc., 1966.

Skulsky, Harold. "On Being Moved by Fiction." *Journal of Aesthetics and Art Criticism* XXXIX (1980), 5–14.

Snow, C. P. *The New Men.* London: Macmillan, 1954.

Strieber, Whitley, and James Kunetka. *Warday.* N.Y.: Holt, Rinehart and Winston, 1984.

Testament. Dir. Lynne Littman. Paramount, 1983.

Threads. Dir. Mick Jackson. BBC-TV, 1984.

Union of Concerned Scientists. *The Fallacy of Star Wars.* N.Y.: Vintage, 1984.

Walton, Kendall L. "How Remote Are Fictional Worlds from the Real World?" *Journal of Aesthetics and Art Criticism* 37 (1978), 11–23.

Wargames. Dir. John Badham. United Artists, 1983.

Waters, Harry F., et al. "TV's Nuclear Nightmare." *Newsweek* 21 November 1983, 66–72.

Wordsworth, William. "Preface to the Second Edition of *The Lyrical Ballads.*" In *English Romantic Writers,* edited by David Perkins, 320–333. N.Y.: Harcourt, Brace & World, Inc., 1967.

Wyden, Peter. *Day One.* 1984. Reprint. N.Y.: Warner Books, 1985.

Wylie, Philip. *Triumph.* N.Y.: Doubleday & Co., Inc., 1963.

Zuckerman, Edward. *The Day after World War III.* N.Y.: Viking, 1984.

Index

DATE DUE

261-2500			Printed in USA